ON BECOMING
CHILDWISE

ON BECOMING

CHILD WISE

GARY EZZO AND ROBERT BUCKNAM, M.D.

Multnomah Publishers® *Sisters, Oregon*

ON BECOMING CHILDWISE
published by Multnomah Publishers, Inc.

© 1999 by Gary Ezzo and Robert Bucknam, M.D.
International Standard Book Number: 1-57673-421-8

Cover photograph by Portlock Productions
Design by David Carlson Design

Scripture quotations are from:
The Holy Bible, New International Version
© 1973, 1984 by International Bible Society,
used by permission of Zondervan Publishing House

Also quoted:
The Holy Bible, King James Version (KJV)

Multnomah is a trademark of Multnomah Publishers, Inc.,
and is registered in the U.S. Patent and Trademark Office.

The colophon is a trademark of Multnomah Publishers, Inc.

Printed in the United States of America

For information:
MULTNOMAH PUBLISHERS, INC.
POST OFFICE BOX 1720
SISTERS, OREGON 97759

99 00 01 02 03 04 — 7 6 5 4 3 2 1

Lance and Susan

Even far away you are close

CONTENTS

Acknowledgments 8

Introduction 9

Summary of Childwise Principles. 12

SECTION ONE: CREATING THE RIGHT ENVIRONMENT

Chapter One: Overcoming Fear. 17

Chapter Two: Keep First Things First 35

Chapter Three: Who's Running the Show?. 45

SECTION TWO: CHARACTER

Chapter Four: The First Principle. 63

Chapter Five: Without This, Character Is Not Taught 75

Chapter Six: Making the First Principle Work 89

SECTION THREE: DISCIPLINE

Chapter Seven: At the Heart of Discipline 113

Chapter Eight: Five Laws of Correction 129

Chapter Nine: The Best Form of Correction—Prevention 149

Chapter Ten: Transferring Ownership of Behavior to Children 173

Chapter Eleven: Encouragement and Correction:
    One Coin, Two Sides 199

Chapter Twelve: Common Discipline Issues 223

Chapter Thirteen: Some Nifty Things. 237

Epilogue 253

Index. 255

Notes. 260

ACKNOWLEDGMENTS

No book is really written by a single author. Neither was this one. We owe a special debt of gratitude to a host of families who walked with us through the completion of this series. We want to especially thank Don Frame for his insightful contributions. We'd also like to thank Tom and Evengline Reed and Allen and Connie Hadidian for their nifty contributions to chapter 13.

We'd also like to extend a special word of thanks to these parent educators: Joey and Carla Link, Michael, Briana, and Amy for their resplendent contribution to chapter 10. And last but not least, we are specially indebted to Diane Wiggins, whose editorial giftedness and genius made this book fun.

INTRODUCTION

On Becoming Childwise, the third in our On Becoming series, targets children aged three to seven years. This is an exciting period of growth and development for children, and a time when parental training and encouragement are major players in the child's developing world. These preschool and early school years awaken within a child a sense of fearful adventure in an ever-expanding world outside the confines of mom and dad.

It is an exciting and, yes, challenging growth period. A time when your child's intellect develops sufficiently to allow purposeful interaction with adults and other children. As that interaction begins, your child starts to process experiences and sensations from his deepening relationships that direct the way he interprets life. As your child's world unfolds, new and broader expectations are realized. Now he is confronted with role functions, norms, and expected standards of conduct which sometimes conflict with each other as well as with his own self-centered perceptions.

Children of this age not only begin to perceive how and where they fit into the larger social picture, but they also develop a life and worldview perception of where everyone else in their mental neighborhood belongs—Mom and Dad, little Kyle next door, and the mechanic down the street.

Our goal is to help you get started and sustain your course of action with confidence. We first want to instill in you a healthy dose of encouragement. The word *encouragement* literally means "to put courage into," and that's what we'd like to do for you. There are so many fearful strategies in the parenting marketplace it is no wonder parents often second-guess their decisions. They fear they are going to do it all wrong and that there is a zero recovery rate from error.

Fear sets in right from the start: the competent nurse hands over your new bundle and wheels you out of her life. This is it. You're on your own. You and about a zillion opinions, regulations, strategies, and bestsellers telling you just what to do now. That's not to mention the other zillion reporting the catastrophic consequences of doing—or not doing—the previous zillion.

One wrong move and you'll break the fragile child. Disposable diapers or cloth? Breast or bottle? Crib or bedside cradle? From rashes to runny noses, bonding to breaktime, everyone—including your neighbor's mother-in-law's friend—has something to say about what you should or shouldn't be doing for your child.

Here is just one word from us: relax. You're going to do just fine, and so are your children. *Childwise* is filled with helpful strategies that will not make you feel guilty or fearful, but will cause you to think through each challenge with that old-fashioned thing called common sense.

We want to give you a renewed sense of purpose in your parenting. What are you hoping for? What is the purpose behind the training you give your child? Your goal needs to be more than just getting through another day. *Childwise* is a values-based parenting strategy.

Parents have an obligation to manage their children, not only at home but also in public settings. *Childwise* stresses the importance of moral socialization as a healthy prerequisite to a satisfying sense of self. There is no greater confirmation of self-worth than appreciation from others. How that is legitimized is taken up in section 2, where we emphasize the importance of character training.

A third aid in the area of confidence concerns matters of behavioral correction. In section 3, we take up the issue of correction and encouragement. While we will discuss many discipline options, we desire that our readers think *prevention* first and foremost. Preventing wayward behavior by not creating the conditions that pull children off-track translates into less correction you will need to do.

Each chapter contains review questions. These are designed to take you back to the major themes found in each chapter. Like anything else in life, the more effort you put into implementing *Childwise* principles, the more help you'll receive and the more confidence you'll gain.

We are excited about offering parents practical helps. Informative books are great for reading, but do little for parents if practical how-tos are missing. We trust you will find *Childwise* informative and highly practical and that the tips actually work, making a discernible difference in your parenting.

Yet at the same time this book is not intended to give all the answers or provide the reader with all he or she will ever need to know about the process of raising a child. Therefore, parents guided by their own convictions have the ultimate responsibility to research parenting philosophies available today and make an informed decision as to what is best for their family.

Be encouraged!

SUMMARY OF CHILDWISE PRINCIPLES

CHILDWISE PRINCIPLE #1
Great marriages make great parents.

CHILDWISE PRINCIPLE #2
*Use the strength of your leadership early on
and the strength of your relationship later.*

CHILDWISE PRINCIPLE #3
Parent now, be friends later.

CHILDWISE PRINCIPLE #4
Instill morality into a child and his behavior will fall into place.

CHILDWISE PRINCIPLE #5
*What you do not yourself desire, do not put before others.
Do to others what you would have them do to you.*

CHILDWISE PRINCIPLE #6
Other people count.

CHILDWISE PRINCIPLE #7

It is not enought to teach your children how to act morally;
they must learn how to think morally.

CHILDWISE PRINCIPLE #8

To teach a virtue, one example (you)
is better than a thousand lectures.

CHILDWISE PRINCIPLE #9

Discipline is heart food for your child.

CHILDWISE PRINCIPLE #10

If learning didn't take place, correction didn't happen.

CHILDWISE PRINCIPLE #11

Allowing a child to progress into his new and
expanding world in an orderly fashion greatly enhances
learning and decreases the need for correction.

CHILDWISE PRINCIPLE #12

Constantly reminding a child to do what is
expected only means you have no expectation.

CHILDWISE PRINCIPLE #13
Verbal affirmation is never redundant.

CHILDWISE PRINCIPLE #14
Wise parenting is better than power parenting.

CHILDWISE PRINCIPLE #15
An ounce of self-control is better than a pound of trouble.

CREATING THE RIGHT ENVIRONMENT

Chapter One

Overcoming Fear

One night, the captain of a U.S. Navy warship saw the light of an oncoming vessel heading straight for him. He signaled ahead: "Change course twenty degrees."

The reply flashed back through the darkness: "Advisable you change course twenty degrees."

The captain didn't accept this response. "I'm a captain," he signaled. "Change course twenty degrees."

The reply: "I'm a seaman second class. Change course twenty degrees."

By this time, the captain was furious. "I'm a battleship! Change course twenty degrees!"

To which came the response: "I'm a lighthouse!"[1]

Assumptions affect our lives. They mold our way of thinking and shape our conclusions. They direct the decisions that lie behind our actions and attitudes. The battleship captain above made an assumption that would have been catastrophic had he not changed his thinking. We rarely evaluate our assumptions, yet we are driven by them. Worse yet, our children often become the victims of our assumptions. Take the case of "Mommy, fetch." A friend shared the following incident:

> I was sitting in a restaurant with a friend and her one-year-old daughter. Now, my friend is no dummy. She graduated from medical school at the top of her class. But I watched her scramble on the floor for little Sarah's bottle again and again. Sarah would throw it and Mommy would fetch it. Throw, fetch. Throw, fetch.
>
> When asked about the appropriateness of this game, my friend responded, "I'm teaching Sarah the concept that if something goes away, it will come back. You see, the bottle goes away, and the bottle comes back. Likewise, Mommy goes away, and Mommy also comes back."
>
> I asked her if she had ever considered the possibility that she is actually teaching Sarah to never expect refusal. To that she responded, "What could go away at this age and never come back?" Sarah provided the answer. At that moment, she emptied her plate of food on the floor, threw the bottle on top of the pile and then smiled. In a moment, she began to scream when the food didn't come back.

Our assumptions affect our parenting. Sarah's mom assumed her daughter possessed a level of cognitive competence—the ability to transfer an idea from one situation to another—that is simply not present in a one-year-old child. She assumed her daughter needed this type of training. She assumed that if she did not instill it, Sarah would be lacking a degree of trust and confidence that could never be recovered. She assumed that the natural process of security development could be manufactured. She assumed the little game of mommy fetch would meet the challenge.

KEEPING YOUR BALANCE

What parenting assumptions do you hold? What are your views regarding children, their natures, and their age-related abilities? Do you feel a child's personality is formed by nature or by nurture? Should parents facilitate a child's timetable of discovery or apply pressure to learn? Are feelings the main thing or is behavior? Natural development or parental training?

We are happy to announce that these are not matters of either/or, but both. *Childwise* recognizes that when it comes to raising children there is a relationship between nature and nurture, facilitating a child's learning and proactively teaching, encouraging right feelings and right conduct, and understanding the relationship between natural development and parental training. It is *yes* to all of them. The only thing parents must wrestle with is the balance.

Consider, for example, feelings versus conduct. We've all witnessed a scene similar to this: The seemingly parentless child wanders up to your child's toy bucket at the swim club and confidently helps himself to a desirable item. You and your child watch as this little wanderer frolics in the pool with his delightful new selection.

Then along comes mom. "Jimmy, where did you get the red boat?" Of course, Jimmy's too enthralled to respond. So, looking around, mom sees your child's eyes glued to the toy. Making the connection, mom turns to you. "Oh, is that your boat?"

You paste on a cordial grin and tell her it is your child's. Certainly, you don't mind sharing, but you do appreciate respectful protocol.

"Jimmy just loves boats," mom says. "Do you mind if he plays?"

No problem, you tell her. All seems well with the world—until it's time for Jimmy to leave.

It seems Jimmy's developed quite a fondness for what has now, an hour later, become his own little tuggy. When mom suggests he give it back, gently reminding her little sailor that the boat is not his, Jimmy simply says no. Mom prompts him again, but his resolve only deepens. So, turning to you, mom tries a new angle. "He really took to that toy. Can I pay you for it?"

Apologetically, you shake your head.

"Jimmy," mom says, "that lady wants it back. Give it back before she comes over and takes it. Don't worry, we'll stop at the store on the way home and mommy will buy you a new boat." Jimmy throws the toy in the pool. Mom walks off. Jimmy pauses just long enough to stick out his tongue at your child.

Have you seen this child lately? What parental assumptions drive such overindulgence at the expense of behavior? Modern parents tend to want to create good feelings in their children at all costs. Getting children to feel good outranks getting them to behave appropriately in the various contexts of life. Such management of children is understandable when considering some of the historical influences on today's parenting.

One of the greatest shifts in Western morality affecting parenting occurred when a group of seventeenth-century philosophers, influenced by a growing respect for naturalism and empiricism, put forth a new proposition. An individual's privately felt pleasure or displeasure, they said, should be the first criteria in judging behaviors good or bad. Noted eighteenth-century philosopher David Hume felt that, "pleasant feelings were good; unpleasant ones were bad."[2] Hume believed that the end of his teachings would be benevolence, an unselfish regard for the welfare of society.

Current parenting theories, which owe much of their assumptions to this philosophy, wash out a bit differently than Hume might have imagined. When converted from theory to lifestyle, these ideas work out to feelings-directed morality and feelings-directed parenting. "If it feels good, do it," this philosophy says. "And if you want to be a good parent, do whatever makes your child feel good."

End of history lesson? Not quite. Today, we live in a day when the "child-centered" ethic has become the grounds for all sorts of overindulgent child-rearing practices—and some even stranger explanations—all to the tune of "pleasant feelings are good; unpleasant ones are bad."

It seems that many parents today are held hostage by fear. Fear that they will not do it right. Fear that the child will become overstressed or overburdened by reasonable demands or disappointments. Even the simple insistence that a toy belongs to another child strikes panic in the hearts of some moms and dads. Look around you. Do you know any parents who are held hostage by fear of emotional reprisal from their four-year-old? Do they seem immobilized, unable to act? Do they ride along the moving treadmill, too afraid to take that small step off? It doesn't have to be that way for them. Or for you.

OTHER FEARFUL INFLUENCES

Why are parents so afraid to parent? Truly, something more significant is going on here than desire to produce the optimum offspring. Maybe some parents are trying to satisfy something deep within themselves that was missed in their own childhood. Many adults do, unfortunately, parent in response to their own unresolved childhood fears, conflicts, and disappointments. As a result, they sometimes parent their *childhood* more than their *children*. They do this by projecting their own fears and disillusionment with life onto their kids.

For example, if your growing-up years were pleasant, there is a strong tendency to use the same training techniques on your children that were used on you. If your childhood years were stressful, your tendency will be to swing to the opposite extreme of your parents' parenting methods when rearing your own children.

Parents brought up under unfair, restrictive, or even abusive parenting methods often unknowingly move toward permissive parenting, allowing their children to become overindulged. Saying, "I'll never let my child go through what I went through," these parents often become more concerned about their children's feelings than their actions. Any standard of right and wrong is based on how their children feel, not what they do.

In contrast, when parents feel that their unhappy childhood was the result of a permissive upbringing, they often become very strict as parents, especially if they feel the lack of guidance was a great handicap to them. For example, those who lived morally relaxed lives in their youth will often overcompensate with their own children by becoming overly restrictive and sheltering. These parents find their security in control.

In both cases, there is a desire to change the status quo, but it is based on fear. Permissive, child-centered parents fear inhibiting their children, so they go to the extreme of creating an environment of unrestrained freedom. No boundaries. This results in undercontrolled children. Authoritarian parents, on the other hand, fear spoiling their children, so they seize the power of rules and limitations. Their methods usually produce overcontrolled children.

The problem is further complicated when parenting styles within the home clash. If one parent is easygoing and flexible and the other structured and predictable, conflict tends to prevail in the home. Each parent considers it his or her duty to compensate for the other's weaknesses. Not surprisingly, each is driven by the fear that the other is not doing it right. Instead of complementing each other by drawing from each other's strengths, as many believe, they actually find themselves at war, playing off each other's weaknesses. The result is divided leadership, producing disloyal troops.

Maybe we are paralyzed by our fear of failure. In a parent's great press for personal fulfillment, a three-year-old's disappointment over a blue sippy cup, a two-year-old's choice to go sleeveless in the

dead of winter, or a teary disbelief that the lollipop within the vehicle is not for instant consumption, all terrify us right into a corner. "If my child cries, people will think I'm a bad parent." With our
collective backs against the wall, we go into survival parenting.

Society has joined against us in force. Containers of candy
await us at every service area. Keep the kid busy chewing and he
many not destroy the store. Not even a trip to the dry cleaners is off
limits: a jumbo jar of peppermints awaits—and hopefully averts—
little Becky's impatient outburst.

No wonder there is a growing demand for "No Candy" lanes,
now available at your local grocer. Forget jumpy Jason screaming
for a Snickers bar! If there's anything mom can control, it's the wallet, right? But only in the "No Candy" lane. If Jason sees the candy,
it's all over.

What's wrong with this picture?

Activities keep us on the run. Tap dance at two. T-ball on
Tuesday. Invitations to parties, house invites, and even sleepovers in
the early years are common fare, the perceived nonnegotiable rights
of the kinder-kids. In between, we make sure we get the kids
logged on, filled in, signed up, educated, and aware. Getting the
toys cleaned up is just too much of a battle with everything else
going on. At this fast pace, who needs the hassle? As for obedience
and honor: not right now. We'll work on that in that hypothetical
day when we'll have time.

Such fear-driven parenting in the early years falls primarily into
four categories: activities, emotions, intellect, and issues of authority. If any of these areas is compromised, the child will supposedly

suffer grievous psychological damage. Fear of messing up their children puts parents on both the offense and defense.

ACTIVITY OVERLOAD

Here's how it works. Too late, you realize your negligence in failing to sign Joey up for toddlers' soccer. You break into a cold sweat. The coach wants to put him on the beginners' team—but he's a whopping six! Fearing severe emotional imbalance, you push for age-appropriate placement, only to discover that Joey has zero coordination. Joey is traumatized by the whole event and grows up to become an operator of the traveling Tilt-N-Twirl amusement ride, where he shouts at patrons and often neglects to push the start button.

Clearly, Joey got left behind, became unglued, and disappeared between the cracks of society. That explains why he has turned rudeness into an art form. If only you had made the sacrifice early on, carting Joey off every Tuesday, Thursday, and Saturday for the endless procession of pseudo-soccer games. The numbered jersey. The feeling of belonging. The cheering crowd. It's all so clear. Joey could have been a winner. But you blew it.

There's more. It was a dream. Your hair is matted to the pillow when finally you awake. Shaking off the memories, you realize this was all a horrific nightmare. No, this can't happen. Not to Joey. He's been in the game since the beginning. He's first string and improving every season.

Still, an uneasy awareness creeps into your being as you head for the fridge. Are you doing enough? Your dream—was it a warning about Joey's future? In the icebox you spy the eggs. That's it. More eggs for Joey, starting tomorrow, and supplements, protein powder, maybe he should be pumping iron before school. You wander back down the dark hall, full of sleepy resolve.

Who's success is at stake here?

By the time kids are five or six, they're saturated with social activities. And still they beg for more! They don't want to miss out on anything someone else is doing. How about that independent six-(going-on-sixteen)-year-old who is already living for the next party? Could she be the one who remarked between mouthfuls of smiley face cupcake that the carnival theme you spent a month planning did not look at all like a carnival to her?

EMOTIONAL ESCAPISM

Take the overly attached mother who feared telling her three- and five-year-old children they couldn't play outside on the swings because it was raining. Instead of refusing them this pleasure, creating disappointment, she disassembled the swing set and set it up in her living room.

Although physically harder, it was emotionally easier for her to do that than to risk what she believed would be a lifelong emotional setback. A single moment of disappointment in the life of her children—one she could prevent. It is not always wrong to prevent disappointment, but such prevention must be realistic.

If this mother's behavior shocks you, consider the number of times you may have disassembled, if not play equipment, then a piece of jelly-covered toast because the child yearned for honey. Maybe you put on Barney sheets when the child preferred that silly ol' bear. Or you reached for the yellow shorts only to discover that purple was the color of choice that day.

In little ways, every day, we disassemble our leadership in order to defer to the tender little wills of our children. Why? Because we fear letting them down. We avoid their bad feelings and pursue their good feelings. This type of parenting only produces emotionally fragile children, children who lack the coping skills necessary for the real world.

If your kids fall apart because they cannot play on their swings during a lightning storm, the root problem may not be your child at all. It may well lie with your parenting assumptions. The mother who rebuilt the swing set is as much a willing participant as a victim. Child-centered theorists have encouraged this type of exaggerated concern about a child's momentary feelings and emotional well-being.

Too often, children are assumed to have adult-level feelings when in fact they don't yet. It is not that parents are wrong to be concerned about such things, but these concerns must be aligned with a child's actual vulnerabilities. If they are not, then protection turns to overprotection, which leads to exaggerated parenting strategies—all to the detriment of the child.

Consider this example:

"Jan, you wouldn't mind too much if Danny went potty outside here by the tree, would you?"

Actually, Jan's dog usually did his business up past the garden, so for a moment, she considered directing little Danny there. But there was another option. "Kath, there's a bathroom right inside the back door, if Danny would be more comfortable."

Too late. Jan looked across the lawn just in time to see four-year-old Danny drop his drawers and squat. Immediately, mom produced tissue to pick up his little nuggets and deposit them in the garbage. Such a tidy woman.

Jan sat amazed, if not a bit nauseous. She eventually worked up the nerve to ask her friend about Danny's issue with toilets.

"Oh, Jan, Roger and I won't erect barriers to his self-expression, or crush his tender little will by insisting he use the bathroom."

The problem with this is that tender little will one day grow up. Then Roger and Kathleen will have a teenager who is used to doing whatever he pleases and letting mom clean up afterwards.

We have great news for parents struggling with a four-year-old's freedom of self-expression: You *can* teach him or her to use the potty without psychologically scarring the child for life. When a child is developmentally ready to be potty trained, do it without the fear of traumatizing your child.

INDULGING THE INTELLECT

Parents feel they simply can't afford to let their child fall behind intellectually. From software for infants to Internet camp, parents want their children to know. Though today's child may not know how to use the potty, most likely he can double-click to select a jolly tune or make the funny rabbit poke out from hiding in the multicolored picture.

Every day, your child receives subtle messages which impact

his or her understanding of the way things ought to be. Sex, suicide, and alternative lifestyles are all acceptable topics today in the educational arena. From extended family to television programming, choices are shaping the child's young mind. The prevalent wisdom states that knowledge gives power. Giving children an understanding of their world is a fine and noble task. But a child doesn't need to know *everything* right now. Where do we draw the line?

ACCOUNTING FOR AUTHORITY

The child-centered parent has an overwhelming fear of holding a child accountable for his or her behavior. That would be a limit to the child's freedoms, a boundary. The parent would supposedly be playing the part of a power-crazed dictator.

At the indoor playground, when five-year-old Erin is told to sit, she says no. Mom is left dumbfounded, wondering where to go from there. What she really wants to do is crawl into a hole, dragging the kid down with her. And to think this sweet lady once fostered dreams of cuddly, tender moments nurturing a respectful relationship with her daughter.

Now Erin's up in the playground tunnels. Mom worries she'll be gray-haired and ancient by the time she'll be able to leave. You see, once the kid's in there, she refuses to let it end. Mom has to hunt her down with a series of threats, persuasions, and, of course, the eventual dangling of candy that she promises "once we're in the car."

In the end, inevitably, she's reduced to cornering the child in the ball pit and leaping forward with a feisty, "Ha! I gotcha!" That's when the tantrum begins. On a good day, it's just whining. Whining is considered mom's lucky break, as it's easily drowned out by explanations to onlookers that the child is extremely exhausted. When they don't buy that one, mom goes to the old standby: "It's my neighbor's kid."

Once in the car, then what? Little Tommy likes to secretly unbuckle himself. Fortunately, modern technology has come to the rescue. Now you can buy the new and amazing Buckle Alert, which catches Tommy in the act and alerts the in-control parent of this dangerous behavior with a series of loud beeps. The only question remaining is, "Now what?" Most likely, for the child needing this mechanism, the alert serves as a pleasant new torture device and source of amusement the entire journey over the hills and through the woods. For mom, this joy ride costs just fifteen dollars (batteries not included).

At home, it's another story. Basements today are a toddler's roost and a prime space for wrecking. Upside-down chairs, mushed crayons covering the floor, dolly clothes left heaped about, and naked Ken and Barbie dolls. Out of sight and out of mind. While upstairs appears to be a palace—shining with mom's elbow grease—the telltale truth lurks below the floor.

We can rest assured that obedience and honor are not top priorities in this household. After all, why bother when there are some nifty instruments of diversion available to eliminate the problems? Tired of the "wardrobe wars" with your child? All you need is thirty dollars to purchase the colorful My Kloset closet organizer, which assists you and your child in planning the entire week's wardrobe in advance. Apparently one major full-blown, all-out catastrophic event on Sunday night is better than daily eruptions. Oh, and mom better hope the weather forecast doesn't send her a surprise storm cloud come Wednesday.

Slamming doors? No problem. Simply slide them off the hinge. Unauthorized snacks eroding mealtime? Easy. Get a padlock for the fridge. Bedtime struggles got you down? When the child collapses on the carpet at midnight, carry the sleeping darling to his lair. Either that or try some bedside television to ease 'em into dreamland.

However, the cause of the problems lingers. At best, happiness at this level is short-lived. As true character begins to emerge later in life, parents are shocked at what they find. Growing beneath their child's appeased facade is a mysterious resentment: contempt, really, for mom's and dad's leadership. This bubbles over in the middle years and beyond.

WHAT DO PARENTS REALLY WANT?

Are there any other parenting goals beyond survival? Someplace down deep in the heart of parents are three universally shared goals. The first: *Parents want to enjoy their children.* We, the Ezzos and Bucknams, enjoyed our children. We enjoyed them in the early, middle, and teen years. We desire that you as reader, mom or dad, will truly enjoy your children. That's the first goal.

However, your own enjoyment of your children is not the only goal. Ma Barker enjoyed her sons just fine. But not everybody shared her maternal joy—they were ruthless killers and bank robbers in the 1920s. If you are looking for one social indicator that measures how well you're scoring in your neighborhood, ask yourself this question:

"Do other people enjoy our children?" The second goal of parenting is *to raise children that are a joy to be with and a blessing to those around them.* Is your child one of those?

The third goal common to all parents is *to raise children who are well-prepared for life.* Will you be able to give your children everything they need to make it in this world—without trying to give them the world? Parents want their children emotionally, intellectually, physically, and morally equipped to enter life outside the watchful and protective eye of mom and dad. On the day your child leaves the nest, will he be prepared to face the challenges of an adult community?

SUMMARY

Every parent wants his or her child to grow up well and to be equipped for life. But sometimes we're paralyzed by the fear of doing it wrong, of committing egregious errors that will doom our children to inferior lives. The good news is children are flexible. They're not that easy to break.

Take heart! There is a way to raise up well-adjusted children who are a joy to others and, yes, to you. The rest of this book is dedicated to showing you how to achieve your parenting goals for your children.

QUESTIONS FOR REVIEW

1. We all hold assumptions about life and parenting. Think through and name three to five assumptions you hold in regard to parenting.

2. What was the major emphasis behind David Hume's philosophy and what impact does it have on parenting today?

3. Many parents today are held hostage by fear. Name some of those fears.

4. What do child-centered parents fear? What do authoritarian parents fear?

5. Name the three universal goals of parenting.

Chapter Two

Keep First Things First

The call for help came at a breaking point. Exasperated and bewildered, Jim was struggling to handle a seemingly senseless nighttime crisis. "Every night, our little Megan wakes up and patters into our room," he said. "Each time, we take her back to her room, tuck her in, and tell her to stay there. It's no use. Thirty minutes later, there's her little face, perched like a puppy on the edge of our bed. Help!"

Cute story? At 3:00 A.M., hardly.

This is the parent zone, where things are not what they seem. Mysterious midnight sightings. A list of broken rules as long as a bungee cord. A child so attached he gives new meaning to static cling. How do you resolve a stream of suspicious behavior? Where do you begin to investigate patterns and uncover the culprit?

Parenting is like a jigsaw puzzle with missing pieces. You have a vague idea of what parenting should look like, but the pieces don't want to fit. Eventually, you try jamming it all into place. In this situation, you might try commands like "stay put" or "stop that." Or maybe you just give up and let the little tyke hop aboard the family bed, sending yourself full speed ahead into marital doom. Eventually you make a realization: the frame of this puzzle is missing a major part. But before you embark on a frantic search of your rules and authoritative reasoning, take a long look at your relationship with your mate.

In the parent zone, the answers to your biggest challenges often lie in this thing called marriage. Marriage represents a special bond between two people that is matched by no other human relationship. It follows that a healthy husband/wife relationship is essential to the emotional health of the children in that home.

Where there is harmony in the marriage, there is stability within the family. Healthy, loving marriages create a sense of certainty for children. When a child observes the special friendship and emotional togetherness between his parents, he feels secure. He doesn't wonder about his parents' commitment to one another. There is no disconnect between what his parents say about their love for each other and what he sees and senses in daily life. Successful parenting flows out of this rock-solid bond.

You probably didn't expect a chapter on marriage in a book about raising three- to seven-year-olds, but we assure you, it belongs. Your marriage is the single most important factor in your child's life. The difference between a child who wonders, "Mom and Dad, do you love each other?" and a child for whom it is never a question is incredible.

What parenting problems a solid marriage doesn't prevent can often be fixed or at least helped by it. The visible health of your marriage affects a child's behavior and his or her sense of love, acceptance, belonging, and, yes, even self-esteem.

YOU WON'T BELIEVE IT

Gary and Anne Marie Ezzo agreed to meet with Jim and Bev, Megan's parents, in their home. There, they observed the family routine at dinner, playtime, and Megan's bedtime. That evening after she was tucked in bed with hugs and kisses, the adults retired to the living room.

"So what do you think?" Jim asked.

"I think," Gary said, "that your daughter is insecure. Something is going on inside that little person. There's something uneasy in her searching eyes."

Jim and Bev fit the profile of a young couple wanting to do their best in parenting. Like others of their generation, they lived with self-induced pressure brought on by the cultural ethic that the child is always first, ahead of everything and everyone else. They believed this formula would ensure a sense of security for Megan. But just the opposite had happened.

Gary asked Jim to recount a typical evening's activities from the time he arrived home from work until Megan went to bed.

"Enter door, greet wife, play daddy for thirty minutes," he said with a degree of pride. "This is Megan's time. We swing or draw pictures. Then, I might tickle her while she giggles and tries to get away. It's all about filling her emotional tank to get us through the evening hours. Then dinner and more time with Megan. Then, after bath, read Megan a story. Finally, bedtime."

Sacrifice? Of course. What child wouldn't want a dad like that? So what was the problem? With such a dedicated routine, what could possibly trigger the bedside visits? Most importantly, how could Jim and Bev fix the problem so everyone could get some rest?

Gary suggested a slight tweak in Jim's nightly routine. Instead of coming through the door and spending time immediately with Megan, he suggested Jim take the first fifteen minutes and spend the time with Bev on the couch, talking about each other's day.

Bev was liking this plan. For Jim it was tougher. He felt Megan would protest this change. She might pull on his arm physically, and emotionally tug at his heart. Still, Gary encouraged Jim to inform Megan lovingly but firmly, "No. Mommy is first. When Daddy is done visiting with Mommy, then Daddy is going to play with you." Though this advice is flatly in opposition to the child-centered ethic of our day, Gary felt it was the very medicine Megan needed. With skepticism, Jim agreed to endure this exercise for a week.

Five days later, the call came. "You won't believe it," Jim said. "After three days of me sitting on the couch with Bev before moving to playtime, Megan began sleeping through the night consistently. Not only that," Jim said, "but now she wakes up happy. Her whole demeanor during the day is noticeably different. The big challenges are gone. What happened?"

Before this change of routine, Megan had only seen her parents acting like husband and wife when they dealt with Megan's midnight visits. There she saw them sleeping together. She saw them working together to try to solve the riddle of her bedside visits. She saw them sitting at the breakfast table together, talking about how they might tackle the problem. In Megan's mind, her nightly episodes were bringing her mommy and daddy together—no wonder nothing was working to stop them.

By displaying this togetherness on the couch (during daylight hours!), Jim and Bev gave Megan what she longed for: the tangible confirmation of her parents' love for each other. At last Megan knew that her world was safe and secure.

A SUBTLE INSECURITY

As professionals, we cannot overstate how necessary a healthy husband/wife relationship is to the emotional well-being of a child. The most basic need of every child is the need to know his world is stable. Every child needs a daily dose of confidence that dad and mom love each other.

Isn't it amazing that even two- and three-year-old children have a radar device that expertly homes in on parental conflict? It is always operative. When a child perceives more weakness than strength in that relationship, he experiences a low-level anxiety that ultimately affects every other learning discipline. This may explain why a child seems to know intuitively—just as you knew when you were growing up—that if something happens to mom and dad, his whole world will collapse. If the parents' relationship is always in question in the child's mind, he will live with emotional nail biting. In contrast, when a child has confidence in his parents' relationship, he is emotionally free to get on with life.

JUST TRY THIS

You must grasp this concept and hang onto it for the rest of this book. We urge you: treasure your marriage throughout your parenting years and beyond. Every phase of your child's development, every behavior, all disciplines of life are impacted by this one special relationship.

Does your child exhibit behavioral problems, moral disruptions, impulsive behavior, talking back, sleep problems, or just outright defiance? Before you do anything else, before you pick up another book, listen to another tape, attend another parenting conference, call your therapist, or get on the Internet—simply practice "couch time" for a week.

As long as you have the couch, you might as well use it. Couch time is free, relatively painless, and has no negative side effects. You will be amazed how this one little exercise can bring peace to a home and emotional confidence to children. Who knows? It may even improve your marriage.

If it does all these for your family, don't ever give it up!

CHILDWISE PRINCIPLE #1
Great marriages make great parents.

When the workday is over, take ten or fifteen minutes to sit on the couch as a couple and talk. Don't watch TV. Don't go through the mail. Talk. Share a dream. Make a plan. You might even make mental notes during the day of little tidbits you could share when you get to the couch.

The only rule, however, is that couch time (chair time, table time) must occur while the children are awake, not after they go to bed. This is the whole point. Explain to your children the importance of having no unnecessary interruptions, because this a special time for the two of you. Explain that dad will play afterward, but mom has his full attention right now—because she's special to him.

If this is a new concept at your house, sit down with your kids and explain what you are about to do. "Today, Mom and Dad are going to sit on the sofa for fifteen minutes and talk. You may be in here if you like if you play with a toy quietly, but you can't interrupt us." Set the boundaries up front. There may be some resistance, some testing of your resolve, but insist.

You will see a change in your children's behavior. Eventually, your little one will remind you when it's time for your chat. They like it that much! And don't be surprised when siblings actually begin their own couch time together across the room.

One other thing about couch time: it's not only for your children's benefit. It provides a forum for a couple to share their relational needs with each other. To visit. For some couples, this time together might be as new for them as it is for their children. You never know, you might just rediscover your best friend.

TROUBLESHOOTING BEHAVIOR

A child's desire for parents who love each other never leaves, not even during adolescence and adulthood. If the two people leading the family can't get along, family harmony can hardly be expected.

Roger and Kim's thirteen-year-old son, Neil, was out of control. It was at a point of desperation that Roger and Kim sought help through a Growing Kids God's Way parenting class. But in order to go to the class, they were going to have to find someone to stay with Neil. Nobody volunteered for the job. And he couldn't be trusted to stay home alone. So each week they brought Neil to the church where the class was being held and sat him in the back of the auditorium, while they sat down front watching Gary Ezzo in the video presentation.

In week three, the topic centered on the husband/wife relationship and a child's need to know concretely that mom and dad love each other. For homework, parents were directed to initiate couch time. But Neil's parents neglected this assignment for three days. On the fourth day, in a moment of crisis, Neil accused his parents of not loving him. "Why can't you give me what I really need? Why can't the two of you just sit on the couch and show me that you love each other? You haven't done one thing that man on the video said to do!"

Apparently Neil was doing more than sitting in the back of the auditorium reading his biker magazine. Out of his own desperation, he was listening to every word of the presentation, hoping for change. It never occurred to Roger and Kim before that moment that even Neil understood this self-evident truth: great marriages make great parents. More than anything they could do or say, their son wanted to know, "Do you love each other, Mom and Dad?" From that moment on, Neil was a changed teen, because his parents started to really love him by demonstrating their love for each other.

There is a widespread myth that kids don't like to see their parents acting mushy. This is simply not true. Children—even teens—thrive on the demonstration of love between parents. Just take a peek over your shoulder while in the clutches of a morning hug. Their little eyes are most likely glued on that embrace. Your beautiful marriage will actually make all of family life attractive.

SUMMARY

When the marital relationship is beautiful, what child would not want to be part of the family? Visually demonstrating your love for your spouse is a win-win proposition. You have nothing to lose and everything to gain. The best years of parenting will flow out of the best years of marriage.

Great marriages make great parents.

QUESTIONS FOR REVIEW

1. How does a child's mind translate seeing parents talking on the couch?

2. How has the child-centered ethic of today impacted the parental view of responsibility to children?

3. What does confidence in mom and dad's relationship enable the child to do?

4. At what age is it too late to establish parent-child trust through demonstrating a healthy husband/wife relationship?

Chapter Three

Who's Running the Show?

*P*arents, let's get this authority thing understood right from the start. You have it. Use it. Don't be afraid of it.

Authority today is a pretty hot area. For three-year-old Billy, the issue flared up after he once again stuck his tongue out at mommy. The next time it happened, mom was ready. She greeted Billy's tongue with a splash of hot sauce. "That really solved the problem for a while," mom said.

But then that old behavior began reemerging at the playground. Such a smart boy. Billy has learned that mom's power is contained in a small red vial in the fridge—at home. No salsa, no authority. What a fun little game.

Certainly, this mother would never classify herself as abusive. She doesn't abuse her son; she only screams at him relentlessly and verbalizes disappointment eternally. Eventually, frustration pushes her to the brink. At three, it's hot sauce. At thirteen, padded room with no key? For Billy or for mom?

Let's face it, authority has been a struggle for humankind from Cain and Abel to Bonnie and Clyde. Children struggle with it from birth, and as we grow older the struggles just grow.

Everybody has an idea for handling authority: diversion, persuasion, surrender, bribery, pleading. One woman, resigned to a lifetime of ornery children, boasted, "I am the self-proclaimed Queen of Idle Threats." The announcement, of course, was not needed. She had threatened her way through ten long weeks of ballet class for her princess. Yet no threat had been carried out. Why was this woman fearful of carrying out a consequence?

For many people, authority has taken on a derogatory flavor. We almost feel like we have to apologize when we use it. "Of course I don't want to ruin his take-charge nature," says one mom, whose two-year-old is attempting to carry his big wheel into the street. "His nature is good, but I want to suppress it a bit."

Truly, an anti-authority attitude can be deadly. When will mom learn that her no must mean no? Hopefully, it won't take a life-threatening scenario to get her little guy into compliance. But it could.

Authority is a necessary positive. Until man can order his own affairs, until he ceases to prey on his brothers, he will need someone to maintain order. This is critical for children. The proper use of authority, whether it be parental leadership in the home or civic government, is not restraint, but liberation. Proper authority restrains only those who would break the laws. It provides freedom for the rest of us to live in peace.

The last half of this century has not been an easy time for parents. As the credibility of more and more expert voices diminishes in the public square, so too does parental credibility and authority.

Proper authority no longer carries with it a legacy of automatic respect as it did fifty years ago. At one time we trusted people in authority. Then in the sixties it became vogue to distrust them. Now we distrust our own understanding of authority.

Maybe this is why authority, parental or civil, is so often abused. In parenting, we find these two extremes: authority is either overused or not used at all. Overindulgent, permissive parents who shun forced compliance look at authoritarian parents and say: "They're too strict! They are stifling the child's creative genius." Meanwhile, authoritarian parents look at permissive households and say, "I don't want my children acting like *that*. Those kids are out of control!"

The parent who controls too little and the parent who controls too much both reflect misconceptions and false antagonism that have misguided today's parents. Though both approaches are attempts to produce conscientious, responsible children, they are extremes which apply improper use of parental authority.

Sadly, many parents live at one of these unwise poles. The over-authoritarian parent may employ highly punitive and sometimes abusive practices which come with strict rules and heavy-handed punishment. The problem here is not the exercise of authority, as some believe, but the excessive and wrongful use of authority.

The child-centered approach is no friend to children, either. Some parents equate overindulgence with love, giving a child everything he wants in the belief that they are teaching some form of benevolence. Withholding correction from the child is equated with teaching a form of heavenly grace. Tolerating disobedience is equated to teaching patience. Diverting a child from sadness, regardless of the root cause of that sadness, is thought to be a form of compassion and consolation.

All of this adds up to a sobering conclusion: imbalances in parenting approaches produce children who are neither a joy to the parents nor a blessing to others. It seems clear that there are many daily occurrences when children require more direction than their self-discipline is capable of producing. To leave children to their whims is to lead them to their own destruction. To be heavy-handed leads to discouragement.

The good news is you do not have to live at either extreme. There really is a balance that works. You *can* parent in a way that not only gets behavioral results from your child, but leaves him happier, more confident, and more contented than ever. That's great news for everyone.

AUTHORITY: THERE IS A TIME AND PLACE

No parenting topic causes greater confusion than the administration of parental authority in child training. Parents and experts alike are polarized over this issue. They shouldn't be. Let us assure you: Parental authority is not a bad thing. Quite the contrary. It is absolutely necessary in order to maintain the balance between personal freedom, responsibility, and obligation.

Parental authority represents the right of parents to insist upon conformity and compliance, especially in these three vital areas of life: morality, health and safety, and life skills.

First, parental authority is necessary to officiate a child's morality. By your authority you lead, guide, encourage, correct, and right the wrongs perpetrated by and on your child. By your moral authority you bring about right moral outcomes.

If your child is rude or discourteous, you work to correct it. If your child selfishly takes a toy from another, you fix the moral transgression. You return the toy to the offended party, and you teach the offender the ethics of private ownership, stealing, sharing, and how to ask for a toy. You also teach in such times the virtues of grace, mercy, forgiveness, and restoration.

You also exercise persuasive authority with health and safety issues. You insist that your child take his terrible-tasting medicine, keep his seat belt buckled, brush his teeth, chew up his vitamins, and take his bath. You call him away from the busy street, the hot stove, and the river's edge. In each case, you insist on compliance.

When it comes to life skills, you insist the cereal bowl be placed in the sink and not left on the table. You enforce a full half hour of piano practice every day. With your authority, backed by your resolve, you insist that the bike be placed in the garage, the homework be done on time, and the dirty clothes be placed in the hamper.

Parental authority represents your right to insist on conformity and compliance for the sake of your child and the benefit of the neighborhood. Can it be abused? Certainly! And at times it has been. Parental authority can be taken to extremes. Too much authority leads to totalitarianism. Insufficient authority leads to social chaos. This is just as true for nations as it is for families.

FROM "YOU WILL" TO "WILL YOU?"

The most important thing about parental authority is that you should be moving toward using it less and less. It should be your goal to come to place where you can lead your child only through your influence. Make this your goal: By the time my child reaches adolescence, I will have exchanged rule-centered leadership for principle-centered leadership.

CHILDWISE PRINCIPLE #2
*Use the strength of your leadership early on
and the strength of your relationship later.*

With young children, lead by the power of your authority. With older children, lead by the strength of your influence. The need for parental authority should decline as your child begins to exercise personal self-control, restraint, and initiative.

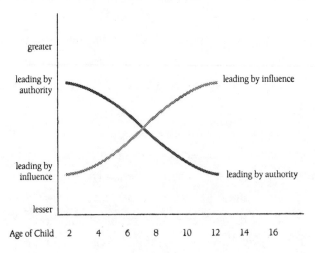

Note the exchange taking place in this graph. In early parenting, parental authority is used to bring about compliance and conformity. But as the child grows, less and less authority is needed to govern. By the time your child hits the late middle years (10 to 12), you will have begun leading by the power of your relational influence.

We can further demonstrate this point by looking at various phases of development. Consider infancy, for example. An infant represents the zenith of parental authority. This is when all of life's decisions are made by mom and dad. You determine when the child will eat, sleep, stay awake, have a bath, play on the blanket, or go for a stroller ride. Such tight supervision is absolutely necessary at this age, since the child simply does not have the moral conscience or intellect to know what is best or necessary.

Now consider parental authority in the life of a five-year-old. By the age of five, a child has gained some internal mastery over his life and actions, and that mastery allows him a corresponding degree of freedom. The decreased need for parental authority is proportionate to the increased amounts of age-appropriate, self-imposed controls. (Please note that parental authority does not diminish, but rather the need for its coercive use does.)

There are some activities in a five-year-old's day that no longer need mom or dad's direct approval. A five-year-old can come and go from the backyard, pick out his own board games, play with his hamster, or go to his room and play with a puzzle. While there is a gate preventing his one-year-old brother from access to the upstairs bedroom, the five-year-old navigates the barrier without need of parental approval. Why? Because the child continually demonstrated responsible behavior in these areas, making parental policing unnecessary.

Our point is this: Although parental authority is still a considerable influence in a five-year-old's life, it is not as sweeping in its control as it was a few years earlier.

How about the child at age ten? Because of his increased ability to govern himself for sustained periods, the need for visible authority is substantially reduced. A ten-year-old should be rapidly approaching moral maturity. Again, it is not that mom and dad's authority is no longer valid, but that the need for external control is diminishing. Gradually, parental *control* is being replaced by parental *influence*. *Extrinsic* motivation governing the child's life is replaced by *intrinsic* beliefs ruling from his heart.

By the time your child enters the teen years, internalized virtues within the heart of your son or daughter should be ruling, not external coercive parental authority. This is where you are headed: adolescence and maturity. Maturity in our three areas—morality, health and safety, and life skills—emancipates the child, allowing him to direct his own behavior in a way you can trust. That is good news for you.

Successful parenting requires full understanding of the proper administration of authority. If you have a three-year-old, do not back away from exercising your social responsibility to lead, direct and, yes, insist on compliance. Lead by your authority when your children are young, guide by your influence as they grow older. Use the strength of your leadership early on and the strength of your relationship later. We'll speak about the means by which parents transfer behavioral ownership to their children in a later chapter.

PAL VERSUS PARENTS

If we are to create a wholesome climate for raising children, we must understand and accept that the first duty of every parent is *to be a parent.* The child-rearing literature of the past few decades has not openly supported this ideal. On the contrary, it has opposed it.

There is a confusing cultural ethic that discourages parents from assuming their leadership role in the family. Take for example the notion of *democratic parenting,* the overly child-centered advice initiated by psychologists and educators, Arnold Gessell and Rudolf Dreikers. Both men rejected the father/mother knows best Judeo-Christian ethic.

Instead, they envisioned future families as small townships in which members of the community could come together, each member with his or her vote to rule on family affairs. Thus, the town council, not parents, runs the family. Every member has an equal vote, including two-year-old Julia. Imagine what this might look like in your home. Perhaps your mind won't allow you to go there.

This is scary stuff. Dreikers, in particular, believed that, since children are equal in human value, neither parents nor teachers have the right to expect or force them into conformity. Carrying this view to its extreme, he believed each child has "the right to decide for oneself, to be self-determining, to refuse to submit to coercion and domination by others," such as parents and teachers.[3]

Dreikers redefined the term *parent* to mean "equal but different." Mom and dad are to be buddies, not authority figures. Proponents of democratic parenting use words such as partnership, equality, and mutuality to describe the parent/child union. We all know it isn't that easy.

Partnership and friendship. What could be more appealing than a family made up of friends? Certainly that is an admirable idea, perhaps appealing to a generation who may have wondered about the absence of friendship with their own parents. But does it really make sense in theory or practice?

CHILDWISE PRINCIPLE #3
Parent now, be friends later.

So many parents today abandon their parental authority in hopes of achieving friendship with their children. What a tragedy, since by doing so they relinquish the very thing that would have given them what they wanted.

Our children are our students. Our role as parents automatically grants us the position of teacher. There will be plenty of time for friendship later, and when parents train correctly, there will be plenty of reason for it. Friendship with our children is not the starting point of our parenting, but the goal. Don't make the mistake of sacrificing your authority for the noble cause of befriending your child. You will get there, but early parenting is not the season for it.

Children need parents who are not afraid to be parents. Why is that? Because children do not enter the world equipped with moral knowledge and life skills. Those are learned. Children do not possess your moral minds or life experiences, your wisdom or self-control of dangerous impulses. Children will receive instruction better from those they respect, authorities on the subject of life, than from peers. You are not your children's peer. You are his parent.

Your children have plenty of friends, but only one set of parents. They need parents who are willing to lead, to insist on compliance, and to show them a safe way. One day, you will bring your children to a common understanding of who you are as a family. You will have communicated to them on many levels what is expected of them and how they need to get along with other human beings with whom they share this planet. On that day, you will be in a position to enjoy your children—and they will have reason to enjoy you. Then you can move into the friend phase of parenting.

FOUR PHASES OF PARENTING

Before the friendship phase arrives, parents pass through three preliminary phases with their children. The success of each phase is dependent on the success of the preceding phase. To successfully pass through them entirely—to truly reach friendship with your grown children—you must stay mindful of each phase: where you are now and where you are headed.

Phase One: Leadership

This phase covers the period from two to six years of age. Your primary goal as a parent in this phase is to establish your leadership in your child's little life. The leadership we speak of is not oppressive, but authoritative. This is a phase of boundaries; boundaries that give way to freedoms as responsible behavior is demonstrated.

This is the boot camp of child-rearing. Your task here is to get control of your child so you can effectively train him. If you cannot control your child, you cannot train him to his full potential, nor will anyone else be able to do so. This phase is the focus of *Childwise*.

Phase Two: Training

The training phase of parenting takes place from ages seven to twelve. To use a sports analogy, a trainer works with an athlete each day in different settings, going through drills and exercises. He can stop the player at any time and make immediate corrections, explaining the reasons and showing him what to do and how to do it. During training, your children are not yet in the real game of life. They are only in practice sessions. This phase is treated in depth in our books *The Smart Parent* and the upcoming *On Becoming Preteen Wise*.

Phase Three: Coaching

The third phase, from ages thirteen to nineteen, is the coaching phase. Now your children are in the game for themselves. We can send plays in from the sidelines and huddle during the time-outs, but we can no longer stop the game for extended periods and show them how it is to be played. The time for training has passed. They now call the plays themselves, adjusting on the fly to what they encounter, and moving forward on their own.

How well you coach your children determines how well they will run the plays of life. But remember, each phase rests on the previous one. Your children will only accept your coaching if you did your job as a trainer. And they will only listen to your training tips if you gained control of them in the discipline phase. If you navigate all the phases well, the transition to the final phase will be a natural.

Phase Four: Friendship

One day you will sit down with your children over a cup of coffee, and all of a sudden you will realize, "We're here." It will hit you that a new relationship is starting: friendship. It is wonderful, liberating, the crown of your parenting. Over the years, you took your wisdom and passed it on to them. You now are morally and relationally netted together in your hearts. You have morally bonded.

There is something very wonderful ahead for you. At the end of your parenting, we want your children to be your friends. Your loyal friends, not just acquaintances. We are fearful for those parents who reverse the process, hoping to cash in now. As with so many things, if you spend it now you may not have it later.

SUMMARY

Gary Ezzo's four-year-old granddaughter Katelynn was digging in her little garden. By her side was a bucket of bright bougainvillea leaves. "What are you doing with those leaves, Katelynn?" Gary asked.

"I'm planting the pretty leaves to grow more pretty leaves."

Gary explained in grandpa terms that the beautiful leaves that give the vine its glory come from seeds and not the pretty bright petals she was putting in the ground. Katelynn thought petals now would mean petals later.

Many parents work from that same misconception, thinking that friendship now will mean friendship later. They see the pretty petals of friendship and want to start there. Unfortunately, it doesn't happen that way.

The process starts by planting a seed. Then you let the seed grow into a sprout. You nurture the sprout until it grows branches. You allow the branches to bring forth their beauty in their time.

In parenting, you start by being a loving and guiding mom and dad who are guardians of your child's soul. At the end of the growth comes the harvest of friendship. The process takes time. Don't rush the fruit.

QUESTIONS FOR REVIEW

1. Name the two extremes of parenting styles prevalent today.

2. What is the ultimate destination goal of your parenting?

3. Take an honest look at where you are now in your parenting. In which of the four phases have you been parenting? Would a different phase be more appropriate?

4. How does parenting in a phase which your child has not yet reached adversely affect him?

SECTION TWO

CHARACTER

Chapter Four

The First Principle

*I*n the mid-1950s, the nation's cultural ethic defined our personal values. It formed the left and right banks of acceptable behavior. Families governed themselves within the framework of a larger moral consensus. Today we live in an age of moral diversity. Each family decides what is right and wrong for them. Frightening prospect.

Such sovereignty has created problems in our schools, churches, synagogues, and neighborhoods—and ultimately our homes, as children struggle through the diversity waiting just beyond the door. If everyone has a different set of values, how do you teach your children right and wrong? And what do you do in the face of so-called postmodernism, which says there *is* no fixed right and wrong? How can you teach them to get along with others? Without a mutual morality, your child may become either a bully or a victim.

For you, our *Childwise* audience, finding moral common

ground that all can applaud will not prove as difficult as it might first appear. We take confidence in the fact that most of our readers share a respect for fundamental character traits. We know you want to instill honesty, empathy, compassion, kindness, gentleness, respect, honor, and self-control in your children.

This is not a wish list from never-never land. It is a reasonable goal for your children. But neither are they born with these virtues. They're cultivated. It is the duty of parents to put character into their children and not sit back and hope good character emerges naturally. It won't.

The aim of this chapter and section is to emphasize the importance of moral education in young children. We desire to show you how young children learn moral lessons, internalize meaningful values, and then translate them into social skills. We want to share with you how to raise great kids; kids who are kind, courteous, respectful, confident, sensitive to others, obedient, fun to be with at any age, and characterized by self-control and cooperation. Simply put: kids who are a blessing to other people. Our goal is to demonstrate that the pathway to a healthy sense of self starts with a healthy sense of "otherness appreciation."

We passionately believe that a child's moral sense proceeds from his early social experiences, directed by parents and influenced by his peer community. That is why it is so important to educate parents. By intent or neglect, parents are still the greatest influence on their children. A pressure-packed statement? Absolutely! Raising good children and having a great family is not a matter of chance—it is parental choice. Even in this age of moral diversity. You, too, can have great kids whose behavior shouts to the world that they have great parents.

What about adolescence? Although this stage may seem eons away, we encourage you to look forward to it with great anticipation, not fear or dread. These years do not have to be stressful nor full of storm. On the contrary, they can, and probably will, be some of the best and most joyful years of your parenting. The *Childwise* principles have demonstrated that outcome repeatedly. You'll get there. It is simply a matter of parenting the whole child.

PARENTING THE WHOLE CHILD

We are pleased to see that within educational circles today there seems to be a healthy movement away from single-focus parenting to a growing consensus in favor of parenting the "whole child."

This term implies a child-rearing approach that considers the natural capacities of children as the primary targets of parenting. It is the counterweight to, on one hand, the unbalanced, child-centered, laissez-faire approach that elevates a child's happiness over morality, and, on the other hand, the strictness of the authoritarian approach that regulates behavior often at the expense of a child's developing emotions.

In the recent past, the title "whole child" has suffered from some myth and misconceptions. Confusion arose over the transliteration of the word *whole* to the word *holistic* as in New Age mysticism. Be assured that neither the word nor the concept has anything to do with such matters. It is a healthy and sensible developmental concept. The essence of the whole child can be measured and understood by the natural capacities of children.

There Are Four General Capacities:

1. Children have *physical* capacities. The duty of every parent is to nurture and provide for his or her children's physical growth and well-being. Parents feed, clothe, and shelter their children and encourage the development of the natural skills and talents necessary for life.

2. Children have *intellectual* capacities. The duty of a parent is to stimulate his or her child's intellectual competency. Parents educate their children in basic skills, logic, and useful knowledge.

3. Children have *emotional* capacities. The duty of a parent is to nurture his or her child's emotional well-being. Parents help their children establish internal controls over both positive and negative emotions.

4. Children have *moral* capacities. The duty of a parent is to help his or her child internalize virtues that reflect the values of the family and society.

All four facets receive attention. None should be neglected, underdeveloped, or overemphasized. Why is that? Because competence and character go hand in hand. You do not want to raise a smart child who lacks integrity. Nor do you want a great athlete with a shallow intellect. Academic skills without values, values without healthy emotions, happy feelings without productivity, and physical stature without moral wisdom all represent developmental imbalances.

A PLAN THAT WORKS

These four capacities—a child's physical skills, intellect, emotions, and morality—are the building blocks of development. All are important, but which is most important? What is the best order in which to arrange them, or does it matter?

The *Childwise* whole child approach assumes that one arrangement of the blocks is indeed better than all others. In fact, disagreement between parenting philosophies usually center on which building block is to be awarded priority in the construction of the whole child.

A small percentage of parents put intellectual stimulation at the top of the pile. Everything else is secondary to the child's cerebral development. When arranging the blocks this way, a child's character and emotions are usually left underdeveloped.

A second arrangement, representing the lion's share of modern parenting thought, considers a child's emotional development as the first priority of training. Morality and academics are dependent on it. The theory is that if children can just be made to feel good about themselves, they will turn out great. (They won't.)

Some parents seem to think physical development deserves the top position. They enroll their children in junior aerobics, peewee football, swim teams, and weightlifting. Certainly parents should encourage their children in this area, but does it really belong in the highest slot? Most kids develop physical skills just by being kids.

How, then, should you stack the blocks? *Place your emphasis on moral training.*

CHILDWISE PRINCIPLE #4
Instill morality into a child and his behavior will fall into place.

We believe moral education should not only be the priority of early training but is absolutely essential for optimal intellectual and emotional development, as well as the advancement of natural skills.

Moral training gives children advanced modes of thought that are more easily transferred to both the intellect and emotions than through any other form of education. Moral training provides the objectivity needed for emotions to function freely without overpowering the child. As a result you are much more likely to successfully parent the whole child. Moral training, done right, delivers the whole package: emotionally balanced, intellectually assertive, morally sensible children, raised to the applause of a grateful society.

Now to come full circle. What should guide your moral training? Specifically, can we establish a singular code of ethics for self and community? Is there a common starting point for morality from which all parental training can be measured and evaluated? We believe there is. We call it the *first principle.* It is the crucial assumption that keeps parents focused on the task, directing and monitoring their children's thoughts, words, and actions.

THE FIRST PRINCIPLE

When asked if there is one word upon which the whole of life may proceed, Confucius replied: "Is not *reciprocity* such a word? What you do not yourself desire, do not put before others." There is a first-century Golden Rule that states the same truth in a positive form: "Do to others what you would have them do to you."

If you want kindness, gentleness, respect, honor, compassion, mercy, and justice shown to you, then live by these virtues yourself. Treat other people the way you want to be treated. Shun the vices of cruelty, selfishness, malice, and deceit. It is never too early to be teaching your children about virtues and vices. But the failure to do so may severely limit his human potential.

Whether drawn from an ancient dynasty or a first-century teaching, the core message is the same: Community life revolves around the assumption that social actions are reciprocal. One's conduct has implications not only toward others but about how we expect others to treat us. Moral reciprocity is a child's teacher. It is fundamental to all relationships. In the past, this ethic is what gave parents moral direction and purpose. It helped them make sense out of their parenting. It still has that same wonderful power today.

The first principle is not the first chronological principle in *Childwise*, but it is the first in magnitude.

CHILDWISE PRINCIPLE #5

What you do not yourself desire, do not put before others.
Do to others what you would have them do to you.

Because morality is fundamentally concerned with one's obligation to others, then everything we do comes back to the first principle. Let your parenting be guided by it. The first principle has everything to do with teaching children how to build and maintain healthy relationships. It starts with this realization:

CHILDWISE PRINCIPLE #6
Other people count.

Other people are precious. Brothers and sisters, mom and dad, grandma and grandpa, cousins and friends—they all count. So does the butcher, baker, and candlestick maker. Everyone in our community matters. Learning how to relate with others is a necessary prerequisite to learning how to feel good about self.

Without a clearly defined first principle, parenting becomes a matter of hit-and-miss. When it comes to subduing mischievous behavior, for example, parents with no first principle tend to look for clever strategies, rules, and techniques. What is the best way to respond when faced with disobedience, tantrums, a finger in the dog's eye, or another missing cookie?

Today's parents have no shortage of suggestions for what to do. "Try a firm no," says one mother.

"Do it with passion," says another. "And if that doesn't work, cry. That always stops my kids in their tracks."

"Just scream," says another mother. "It works for me."

"I persuade my children," says another mom. "I talk to them gently and calmly, reasonably explaining the situation. If that doesn't work, I get the wooden spoon. That works, too."

If none of those solutions work, the modern parent can farm the kids out. Let the sitter, the nanny, the teacher, or the neighborhood kids deal with the issue.

Ready for a better idea? Go back to the first principle. If you operate from a first principle orientation, the discipline technique you use becomes secondary. The question, "What am I going to do in this situation?" becomes less difficult. Everything snaps into focus when you ask your child: "Would you like someone to treat you like you just treated Jennifer?"

The first principle is your guide. You must feed it, satisfy it, live by it, monitor behavior by it, and cultivate it in your children. It is your rudder, your compass that always points true north. When the first principle is transferred to children, it becomes their guiding light, helping them transition from their natural self-orientation to an otherness perspective.

How does this proposition square with all the self-esteem training of our age, which emphasizes self rather than others? It doesn't! Isn't that a relief? Everyone is looking for the cultural antidote to natural selfishness. Enhancing self-esteem is not it. We serve our children better by helping them acquire the values and virtues on which a positive sense of self is actually built. Without a healthy otherness ethic in place, there is no basis for self-respect, let alone any basis for personal esteem. For the latter grows out of the former.

I (Robert Bucknam) see this in my practice all the time. Moral error fuels disappointments. Disappointments fuel discouragement. Children have difficulty feeling good about themselves when they lack the social and moral skills necessary to get along with others.

BENEFITS OF THE FIRST PRINCIPLE

We will endeavor throughout this book to show you the practical side of moral training. The everyday how-tos. We're excited about this because we know when a principle is made practical, beautiful changes come into the lives of children. In fact, parents today have every reason to hope for and experience strong, positive, healthy, and lasting relationships with their children.

The benefits of right moral training derived from this first principle are inspiring. Here is a short list, drawn from families who have employed the "treat others as you would like to be treated" first principle. This is a sampling of what we believe can happen with your children.

The first principle ethic:

- if established during the preschool and elementary school years, becomes the basis of self-assurance and relational success during the teen years;
- is the foundation upon which emotional, intellectual, and creative ventures flourish;
- gives a child the best chance of growing into a happy, well-adjusted, and successful adult;
- provides the armor that protects kids from drugs, alcohol, unhealthy habits, and delinquency;
- is often associated with high motivation and drive for achievement in school, work, and play;
- helps children develop high moral standards, have deeper relationships, and have more friends who are honest;
- produces children who stand strong and will not succumb to peer pressure;

- produces children who are more open to constructive criticism;

- produces in children closer relationships with siblings, parents, and grandparents; and

- draws appreciation from those outside the family—teachers, coaches, and employers.

If these are not enough to convince you, consider your alternatives. If the first principle really is what provides children the relational attributes listed above, then what happens in its absence? Our playgrounds and grocery stores—and our jails and talk shows—are full of examples. The stakes are high in the arena of parenting. Success or failure is seen in results only measurable ten years down the road. Choose your child's future wisely.

QUESTIONS FOR REVIEW

1. What is implied by the phrase "parenting the whole child"?

2. What are the four building blocks of a child's developing world? Which should take priority and why?

3. In your own words, describe the first principle.

4. What parenting style is the major rival to first principle parenting? Explain any associated problem.

Chapter Five

Without This, Character Is Not Taught

O ne of the first challenges for parents is to discover what
character traits they desire to see in their children. They
also need to determine what traits they don't want to show
up. This process is often facilitated by observation: We see attitudes
we like and attitudes we don't like in children all around us.

Think about the teens you know. We have all met teens, pre-
teens, and even younger children with whom we enjoy spending
time. They are sociable, courteous, respectful, gracious, motivated,
and genuine. They come from families where love between parent
and child is evidenced by their mutual respect for one another and
by the absence of rebellious conflict.

How did these families get to the place of relational harmony?
What is it about these kids that make being with them enjoyable?
What allows you to have fun with them (and them with you) with-
out having to stoop to a buddy status? There seems to be a common

thread between them: These children possess a moral maturity. How do you get there with your kids?

ELENA'S STORY

On one occasion, Gary Ezzo interviewed eight-year-old Elena, who was seeking entrance to a private school. To maximize educational excellence, the administration of this school was as concerned about moral readiness as they were with academic preparation.

Gary posed a hypothetical moral question to Elena: "If you were sitting on a bus and all the seats were taken, and an older person came on the bus looking for a seat, what would you do?"

Elena put her head down for a moment, processed the question and then offered this response. "It all depends," she said. "If there was a sign on the bus that required children to stay seated while the bus was in motion, then I would scoot over and ask the person to sit next to me. But if there was no sign, I could get up and let the person have my seat. Both ways, I could honor age."

Elena's answer is amazing on a number of levels. But what is perhaps most astounding is her introduction of a new element: a sign requiring that children remain seated while the bus was in motion. By adding this element, she created a condition in which two competing values of equal weight called for Elena's simultaneous attention: obedience to authority, represented by the sign, and respect for the elderly, derived from her parents' Judeo-Christian heritage. In the face of these seemingly conflicting values, her eight-year-old mind processed all the variables and came up with a way to satisfy both values without compromising either.

How is such moral insight gained? And what role do parents play in cultivating or delaying healthy moral attitudes? Here are six precepts of moral development.

Moral Precept #1:
Teach the Way of Virtue, Not Just the Avoidance of Wrong

Studying child-rearing patterns over the years, we have discovered that parents tend to spend more time and energy suppressing wayward behavior than elevating good behavior in their children. That is, when teaching moral principles, parents will often tell their children what is wrong and what not to do, rather than what is right and what they should be doing instead.

This type of training leads to serious moral compromise in the future. Because so much emphasis is placed on which behaviors to avoid and too little on which ones to pursue, the path to virtuous deeds is left undefined for the child. If all you do is describe bad behavior, then the only thing your child has a mental image of is bad behavior.

Certainly Elena's mom and dad understood the importance of suppressing her self-oriented, wayward behavior. That's a significant part of child-rearing. But they also understood that if they only suppressed wrongs and did not elevate right behavior, ultimately they would end up distorting the meaning of "good" in Elena's mind. Restraining wayward behavior is the left hand of parenting, describing and encouraging admirable behavior is the right.

Eleven-year-old Sandy tormented her younger sister, Cheryl, in many unkind ways. Sandy would tell her friends secrets, but she would publicly exclude Cheryl from these private murmurs. When the two girls rode bikes together, Sandy would cause Cheryl to fall off and get hurt. Sandy would manipulate situations to gain an advantage over her sister, often at the expense of her sister's feelings. The girls' mother corrected each occurrence by punishing Sandy, but could not understand why such exaggerated one-sided sibling conflict continued.

This mother failed to realize the principle above. Yes, she temporarily suppressed Sandy's waywardness by correcting each occurrence, but that's what led to the perpetual problem. She focused so much on unkind behavior that she failed to teach the necessity of being kind. She did not provide Sandy with another model of behavior, a picture of what kindness to her sister might look like. She was reactive when it came to wrong but not proactive when it came to teaching that which is right and virtuous.

Sandy needed clear instruction and encouragement in demonstrating love for her sister. Suggestions for exhibiting kindness were critical for this older sibling. Could Sandy reach out with a hug for her little sister each morning? Could she take time to demonstrate a new skill? Could she do a craft or play a game suggested by her sibling?

Restraining morally wrong behavior and encouraging morally right behavior are two sides of the same coin. Both must be taught by parents if a child is to reach moral maturity.

Moral Precept #2: Moral Training Begins in Parents' Hearts

Moral training begins with mom and dad. Effective parents know they cannot lead their child any farther than they have gone themselves. If the prescription for moral living is not written on the parents' hearts, it will never be passed on to the children.

Bear in mind that a parent with advanced moral knowledge is not automatically a moral person. A moral lifestyle is not the automatic result of moral knowledge; it's a separate package entirely. Knowing right from wrong and doing it are different things.

Personal integrity remains one of the great credibility builders of parenthood. Hypocrisy, on the other hand, will smash that credibility every time. Parental hypocrisy occurs when mom and dad exempt themselves from values they require of their children. It's a breeding ground for contempt.

The moral rules we require our children to follow must also apply to us. There can be no double standard in the upright home. A father cannot lecture on honesty and then, when the phone rings, say to his wife, "Tell them I'm not home." A mother mustn't require that her child respect authority, then go ballistic when a policeman pulls her off the road for driving too fast.

The truth is, our children will live at the same moral standard we do, no matter what standard we describe with our lips. As parents, we must be continually growing in our own moral sensitivity. Actively applying virtues and values in our own lives legitimizes the instruction we give our kids. This is important because in the years just around the bend, your kids will be watching every move you make. Slow down and take a moral inventory.

Moral Precept #3: Know the Why of Moral Training

Many children know how to apply moral law but not as many know why it's correct. Knowing *how* to do right and *why* they should do it are two distinct entities. The first represents an action; the second represents the principle behind the action.

Often children are taught what they should not do (e.g., do not steal) or should do (e.g., share your toys with your sister). However, parents in our society consistently fail to teach the moral or practical *why* of behavior. This results in children who are outwardly moral but not inwardly. They know how to respond in different circumstances because they have been trained, but they cannot adapt to unforeseen situations because they do not grasp the underlying moral principle.

Like Elena, seven-year-old Robby went through a moral readiness interview at the same private school. "Robby," the administrator said, "imagine that you and your family are eating dinner at Mr. and Mrs. Brown's house. After dinner, Mrs. Brown brings out a beautiful cake and starts to pass out pieces to everyone, including herself. She then takes the cake and returns it to the kitchen. When would you start eating your piece of cake?"

"After Mrs. Brown sat down and started to eat her dessert." His answer speaks to the moral behavior insisted upon by his parents.

Next the administrator asked a more specific question: "Robby, tell us, why you would wait?"

What would you expect his answer to be? Something along the lines of, "Because that's the way my parents taught me to do it," perhaps. But Robby's parents had taught him the *why* of moral behavior. "My parents taught me that love is not rude," he said. "It would be rude not to wait for the one who served us."

Here is a child who is in the process of becoming morally mature.

CHILDWISE PRINCIPLE #7

It is not enough to teach your children how to act morally;
they must learn how to think morally.

If a moral virtue is to take hold within a child, it must be placed there. Then the child must actually interact with the virtue. Little is accomplished by a one-way lecture about how a child should act.

Does this precept obligate you to provide a *why* explanation every time you correct your child? Of course not. There will be plenty of times in the early years when your explanation is simply, "Because Mom said so." But by the time your child hits three years of age, instructions that are tied to moral behavior should include moral or practical reasons why.

Moral Precept #4: Provide the Why of Practical Training

Not every explanation offered by parents will be associated with moral training. Some explanations serve only a practical purpose. As a general rule, parents should offer a moral reason when a situation concerns people, and a practical reason when a situation relates to things. In some cases both are joined together.

Four-year-old Sean just couldn't resist. The temptation was overwhelming. While walking through the grocery store, Sean became fascinated with the black and white plastic shelf labels staring him in the face. He found it amusing to slide each bold number back and forth in its track, bunching them together into little trains. His mom tried every trick in her discipline bag, but nothing worked. Finally, she gave him the practical reason why. "Sean, if you move the price tags, the people coming behind us will not know how much to pay for the things they need to buy."

That simple explanation had a profound impact on this small child. It was both moral and practical—politeness for others coming behind (moral) and preventing pricing mistakes (practical).

This triggered something in Sean's mind. His mom and dad had managed their lives, home, and children according to our first principle: treat others the way you want to be treated. Since his family was already other-oriented, mom's reason fit naturally into Sean's worldview. Not moving the price tags made perfect sense to this little guy—doing so would be rude, mean, and disrespectful. He even communicated that principle to his little three-year-old sister, encouraging her not to touch the numbers. Sean took personal ownership of his parents' values.

That ownership comes as a result of several factors working in harmony to achieve the goal. Ownership starts by instilling your values into the heart of your child. The process also includes parental example, trusting relationships, parental honesty, security of the husband/wife relationship, the expression of family loyalty, and many more relational components. All of these factors encourage your child to integrate mom and dad's value system into his or her life.

Here is another example of a practical *why* explanation. Shayla's dad was working on a weed problem near the fruit tree. His busyness attracted her curiosity. Seeing his daughter draw near, he warned, "Shayla, move away from the tree. I just sprayed poison around the trunk, and it's not safe."

In this situation, there was a practical reason (health and safety) why Shayla's behavior needed to be restrained, not a moral one. Since Shayla received practical information about what was going on at the tree, her curiosity was not further enticed. That information minimized the tension between Shayla's need for obedience and her natural curiosity. Her dad satisfied her childlike need to investigate.

Moral Precept #5: Make Moral Judgments by Examining Context

After morning services, four-year-old Stevie was running recklessly on the church patio. Stevie's dad, observing the crowd, suggested to his wife that Stevie should stop. But Stevie's mom said, "He's just being a boy."

Is there a moral issue in this scenario that should be acted upon? Is there something intrinsically wrong with running? Of course not. Let's look closely.

We cannot classify an action as acceptable or unacceptable without first placing it in its context. The context of any given situation allows a parent to focus on the right response without compromising moral truth. Context is what helps determine whether an action complements or detracts from our moral convictions.[4]

A little boy running may appear to be a morally neutral event. But when you put his running into context—a patio filled with elderly people, younger children, people in wheelchairs, mothers with babies—Stevie's behavior is no longer morally neutral, but morally unacceptable. Stevie's behavior demonstrates a lack of concern and respect for the welfare of others. It violates the first principle. It is his parents' responsibility to stop him from running and explain to him why.

In contrast to Stevie, Chelsea stood close to her parents' side. Although she wanted to join Stevie's play, they said she could not. Chelsea's parents lived by the *Childwise* first principle. They explained to Chelsea why running was not appropriate on the church patio at that time. They considered the welfare and feelings of others and made a judgment as to what would be the most appropriate behavior under the circumstances. Then they explained their decision.

Rather than issuing a sweeping command like, "Don't run," they trained her in action and principle. By teaching her the principle behind the decision, they taught her to be morally discerning. When a similar situation presents itself in the future, Chelsea will be prepared to respond according to the principle she learned here.

Let's extend this hypothetical example to make this crucial principle doubly clear. What would have happened if Chelsea's parents had not given her the reason for their restriction? Think about a situation this week in your own parenting in which you restricted your child with some form of no, but left it at that. As it relates to child-rearing, we have consistently found that today's no is only for today. The child does not understand the wrongness of his actions.

Without the moral *why* today, then when a similar situation presents itself tomorrow, the morally uninformed child has no good reason not to run. Why is that? Because no reason has been placed in the heart. If there is no moral precept to stir the heart, the heart will not be stirred. Why do children seem to repeat offenses? One reason may be the absence of moral reason. "No" stops an offense only temporarily.

Moral Precept #6: Avoid Legalism When Giving Instruction

If you're a *Babywise* parent, you will remember this warning. In an attempt to ensure moral compliance, some parents go to the dangerous extreme of labeling every behavior either right or wrong, without any consideration given to context. Making such sweeping statements is neither accurate nor appropriate.

This is legalism country. Legalism elevates method over moral principle to create prohibitions. When we value the law more than we do grace, we succumb to legalism. Legalists tend to see all decisions in life as either good (moral) or bad (immoral). If you do something wrong, even accidentally, it is considered *bad*. And, by the way, so are you (bad, that is, since legalists often equate behavior with worth).

The most notable habit of a legalist is rejecting context. Responding to the context of a situation does not mean we've lapsed into moral relativism or that we should suspend law or principle. It means we should apply them in the most appropriate way. We hold to the *spirit* of the law. Considering context guards us against legalism.

Let's go back to Chelsea and her parents. What if they had said, "Chelsea, while at church you are *never* to run on this patio"? Do her parents really mean "never"? What if Chelsea was called upon to get the church nurse or doctor for an emergency? Could she run under those circumstances? What if there was a fire? Your child is better served by knowing the principles behind the law than simply knowing the letter of the law.

SUMMARY

In addition to teaching children how to act morally, parents must teach them how to think morally. To accomplish that goal, parents also must think and act in accordance with fundamental values. Thinking is the prerequisite to the process of raising a morally responsible child.

The lack of any predominant standard for moral excellence in our society threatens each subsequent generation. As each generation becomes more desensitized to the value of others, we will inevitably raise up a generation that will mark the point of no return. What one generation will allow in moderation, the next will allow in excess.

QUESTIONS FOR REVIEW

1. When teaching moral principles, parents will often tell their children what is wrong and what not to do, and forget to talk about what is right and what they should do. What is wrong with this practice?

2. In our story about Sandy, what mistakes did her mother make as she tried to suppress Sandy's wayward behavior?

3. What is one of the most destructive forces in parenting, as described in moral precept #2? Explain.

4. What is the difference between knowing *how* to do right and *why* it is right?

5. Explain in your own words the importance of context.

Chapter Six

Making the First Principle Work

M egan is shy. She can barely look you in the eye. As for saying hello, well, you just can forget it. Sometimes this makes for awkward situations, but you suspect she'll outgrow it. She'll just never be an enthusiastic communicator. Some things you can't change.

How about Ben? Sure, he'll say hello. He'll also show you the loose tooth hanging on by a blood-covered thread. He's a cute little fella. And smart! He knows everyone by first names. So he calls the elderly couple across the street Bob and Jean, and his teacher at preschool is, simply, Linda.

Maybe you recognize this child. Maybe it's the kid next door or your child's playmate. Then again, maybe it's live and in full color: the kid by your side. Certainly a child is born with a particular temperament on which personality is built. However, these do not excuse a child from appropriate character training. The combination of virtues instilled in a child's heart must be the same, whether the child is Megan, Ben, or yours.

But there is more to character than shyness and loose teeth. Character, in fact, is not about a person's temperament or personality. It is the quality of a person's personality and the moral restraint or encouragement of his temperament. It is the outward reflection of the inner person. Our character reflects our morality and our morality defines our character. They are inseparable.

When it comes to character training and children, do not assume for a minute that all you have to do is sit back and let all that good character naturally bound up in the heart of a child ooze out. On the contrary, parents build character *into* their children—not draw it out.

It's a process that parents must take ownership of. You can sit your child under the tutelage of a piano teacher, T-ball coach, ballet instructor, or Sunday school teacher, but when it comes to character training, mom and dad are the chief shapers of his heart. By three years of age your child's heart and mind are ready to learn—you must be ready to teach. The intellect is budding and emotions are ripe, making the child ready to receive moral impressions.

Be patient as you tweak the heart of your child for optimum function. Like a highway construction project, parenting is never completed quickly enough for our satisfaction. Training the reason why right is right and wrong is wrong into the heart of your child takes persistence and patience, along with a clearly defined plan. Allow extra time for major delays not to mention unexpected speed bumps and a shortage of support crews.

BUT MY CHILD IS DIFFERENT

Perhaps you're thinking, "But children are all different! How can you expect the same thing from every one of them?" Our answer is that character transcends natural differences.

When it comes to children, temperament and personality are the variables of training. Every child receives a different measure. Every child has a unique combination of abilities, weaknesses, aptitudes, learning styles, temperament, and personality, and all must be considered. However, do not assume character training is dependent on temperament. Virtues are absolute and not swayed by temperament. When it comes to character formation, how children learn will vary. *What* they are learning must be the same.

Think of it this way. If you take twenty people and put them in a room, you will end up with a smorgasbord of personality and temperament combinations. Which of the twenty personality types in that room should be exempt from kindness, patience, self-control, gentleness, humility, endurance, obedience, respect, honesty, or integrity? None, of course. When it comes to the standard of ethical training, one size fits all.

Neither temperament, personality—nor even gender ("he's all boy," "girls are just moody")—may be used to excuse rude behavior or disobedience. Parents should not lower the standard to fit the child, but train the child to rise to the standard. We teach, encourage, affirm, correct our children; and we live the standard ourselves. But we do not dismiss the standard based on the child's temperament.

PRACTICAL VIRTUE

Virtues are like lightning bolts: they're almost impossible to describe, but when you're near one, you know it. How do you know if you are raising a thoughtful, courteous child? What do gentleness and respect look like practically? Kindness, gentleness, love, respect—all are simply abstract concepts to children. To be learned, to be internalized, the abstract must be made concrete. Parents do this through practical, everyday examples.

CHILDWISE PRINCIPLE #8
To teach a virtue, one example (you)
is better than a thousand lectures.

Parents must show their children concretely what these virtues look like everyday. The intent of this chapter is to demonstrate the practical side of moral training. We'll give ideas about how to make the abstract concrete in three major areas: property rights, respect for age, and relationships with peers and siblings.

RESPECT FOR PROPERTY

Other people count. We've established that. But there's a second part to it: other people's stuff counts, too. Teaching your children to respect the property rights of others is an important facet of moral training.

The notion of private ownership goes way back. The Jewish record reveals both Cain and Abel brought the fruit of their labors (i.e., private property) as offerings to God.[5] The eighth commandment states, "Thou shall not steal."[6] According to this edict, God himself promoted a property rights ethic. Back then and today, "Thou shall not steal" means we are not to take another man's money or possessions or defraud him by preventing him from receiving what is due. Regardless of your religious affiliation, you have to appreciate the command, even if the only thing you own is a ballpoint pen.

Teaching respect for property begins at home. When the Bucknam and Ezzo children were very young, we took seriously the task of training them to respect the property of others. We started in our living rooms by setting boundaries both for their welfare and our peace of mind. Certain items were simply off limits to their touch. This in no way impaired their healthy psyches or stifled their creativity. On the contrary, we would argue this training helped bring out the best of both.

When visiting friends, we did not rearrange their living room, claiming that the items were too tempting for our children. Our children did not explore bedrooms, open cabinets, the refrigerator, or dresser drawers. That would have been rude. We didn't child-proof our home or anyone else's. Instead, we morally house-proofed our children.

As parents, we were guided by our first principle. "What you do not yourself desire, do not put before others. Treat others with the same respect you desire be shown to you." Our training was motivated by our ethical responsibility to respect the property of others in the same way we would like our own property treated. We desired that our home be a fun place to visit, but equally a place respected by others, and we are sure you desire the same thing for yours. Therefore, the standard we seek from others is the one we insist on with our children. It is part of our broader social obligation.

More than that. A child's sense of self-approval and esteem is greatly enhanced and reinforced when they overhear, "My, Ruth, your kids are so respectful. They can come and visit anytime."

This type of training was not a quirk of the Ezzo or Bucknam families. It was a generational response—a socially understood, accepted, and expected standard of training in that day. Respect for property was a visible virtue of the American culture. The rights of others not to have their property inappropriately touched by untrained children was more important than allowing a child's impulsive desire to be satisfied. Their desire to touch would be satisfied at the right time under the appropriate conditions. A neighbor's home afforded neither of these.

Value the Person or the Property?

Teach your children that it is the owner, not the thing owned, that is to be respected. Viewing the owner as the object of respect eliminates independent value judgments that lead to conditional respect. For example, the condition of your front lawn, whether beautifully groomed or overgrown, has no bearing on my obligation to respect it. I should not toss my gum wrapper on your property, even though it would never show up amid all those weeds. Ultimately, what evokes my respect is the property owner, not simply the property.

Do you assess the value of an item based solely on its use? Consider a grocery store shopping cart, for example. Typically, they are left everywhere except where they belong, so that they become a nuisance taking up parking spaces and frustrating the people who come along later. Can you control the wind? Are you willing to accept responsibility for a runaway cart or a scratch or dent damage done to another car? Imagine returning to your car only to find two carts pushed against it. How would you feel? Probably violated.

Think about doing something wonderfully countercultural. Take your shopping cart back to its proper place. Make it a moral habit for your family. And when teaching your children the why of your behavior, remember that taking a shopping cart back to the front of a store is not the virtue—respect is the virtue. Returning the cart is one possible way to *demonstrate* what the virtue looks like practically.

Finally, when your children ask why you are suddenly taking back your shopping cart, especially when nobody else is doing so, say, "Right is right, even if no one else is doing it. Wrong is still wrong, even if everyone else is doing it." That is one of the mottos of a first principle family.

Labor Defines Value

The best way to teach children the value of property—theirs or another's—is through labor. Their respect for the value of property is greatly enhanced when children are given opportunities to work. It also will be more quickly internalized. That is because universally, labor defines value.

Labor is what gives meaning to a dollar. The child that labors to earn money to purchase a bike will have a greater appreciation for its value than the child that receives it as a gift. The sense of stewardship in the child who worked will be greater than in the child who didn't, since the value of the bike is closely related to labor.

We are not implying that parents should never buy gifts for

their children. But we are offering this warning: A child who grows up getting things he wants just because he's a sweet person will have an unconscious expectation that the world operates this way, too. "I should just be given what I want because I'm a nice person." The hard realities of the world—i.e., no work, no pay—may send the grown child into a tailspin or cause him to seek ways to continue getting things for free, "just because."

We divide labor into two categories—duty labor and purchasing labor. Laboring out of duty relates to an individual's responsibility to the family. This is the realm of chores: feeding the dog, bringing in firewood, setting the table, taking out the trash, and doing the dishes. Duty labor is not done for money but to help the team. Everyone does something in support of the family.

Purchasing labor is work done for financial compensation. This occurs when a child seeks a job with the goal of purchasing something specific. That type of labor gives real value to money. When the Ezzo children were seven and nine, they desperately wanted a popular board game that cost twenty-five dollars. They came to dad seeking a job. Gary joyfully offered to pay them one dollar for every five-gallon bucket of rocks they picked out of the garden and dumped on the rock pile thirty yards away. They agreed.

At first, it seemed an easy way to earn money. The rocks were plentiful. They filled up the bucket with glee. But then they made a sickening realization: They couldn't move it. So instead of twenty-five trips to the rock pile, there would be fifty trips with half-filled buckets. Two weeks later they earned their money and bought that game. No toy ever received quite as much attention and care. Why? Because their labor gave that board game its value.

From that one experience these children completely grasped the value of a dollar. You know what a dollar is? A dollar is one full bucket's trip to the rock pile. When our kids went out to purchase something that was twenty dollars, thirty dollars, forty dollars, or fifty dollars, they knew what it meant. A twenty-dollar dress was forty trips to the rock pile. The value of the dress now had real, concrete (more like gravel, actually) meaning. More than that: They suddenly could see the true values of a friend's dress, a car, or a house and everything in it.

Your children do not need to pick rocks to learn this lesson. There are plenty of extra jobs around the house. All kinds of things need washing: puppies, cars, windows. Just keep it age appropriate. Somewhere along the line make sure your kids learn that the real value of a dollar is not what it can buy but how hard they had to work to earn it. When they do, they become great respecters of other people's possessions.

Of course, teaching respect for property begins many years before a child is old enough to work for hire. Remember the basics. Do not let your children throw another child's toy, play behind your neighbor's curtains, jump on the furniture, or in any other way disrespect your property or anyone else's. And be sure to teach them the otherness "why" behind your restrictions. Other people's stuff counts.

RESPECT FOR AGE

If there has been anything crucial lost in our society over the last half of this century, it has been respect for age. In the past, parents taught their children to respect their elders. Age was an honored institution. Today, our society barely tolerates the elderly among us. Tomorrow, if no change comes, we will view the elderly as a burden on society. The next logical step beyond that is to exterminate the elderly. And don't forget: Sometime in there *we* will be the elderly.

Youth and Age

When an adult and a young person reach the door at the same time, what should be the response? Youth should honor age by allowing the adult to go first or by opening the door as a courtesy. This is a simple gesture, but it reflects an attitude of respect and honor.

Here is another example. At the church, synagogue, or family gathering where food is presented in a buffet setting, consider inviting the elders among you to go through the buffet line first. It is a small gesture but one that sends a wonderful message to your children. How about teaching your children to honor age by giving up their seat when there are no other seats left, such as on the bus, in a crowded auditorium, or in your living room?

These are moral courtesies you may have grown up with. Pass them on to your children. Respecting age in this manner is not old-fashioned. It is a type of moral example that is never out of vogue. Insisting upon these actions—and teaching the principles behind the lesson—help in the process of cultivating right actions and beliefs in your children.

Our Actions Should Never Be Rude

Why shouldn't children chew their food like a barn animal or spit on the sidewalk? Why should children respond to others when spoken to? Here is one ethic flowing from our first principle that we hope all *Childwise* children become characterized by: Our actions should never be rude. The virtue corresponding to rudeness is courtesy. Teach it to your children.

The Interrupt Courtesy

We have all been there before. There are few disrespectful actions worse than having a conversation rudely interrupted by a demanding child jerking on mom or dad's arm insisting on an immediate audience, and totally disregarding the context into which he is stepping. There is a better way. Teach your child how to interrupt your conversation politely. This is another practical way of showing respect to others. There is a simple technique which eliminates this problem.

When your child needs to interrupt, teach him to place a hand on your side, shoulder, or arm and then wait the few moments it will take for you to acknowledge him. From the child's perspective the hand on your side silently means, "Mom, I realize you're talking with someone else, but when you get a moment, may I ask you something?" This will work if the child knows that you will indeed find a place in the conversation to politely say, "Excuse me," to the person you are speaking to and give the appropriate attention to your child. Win-win. This gesture beautifully displays respect for you and the one to whom you are speaking.

Also, when your child puts his hand on your side, take your hand and place it on his, gently squeezing it. This lets him know that you know he is there. Often, the reason a child pulls on the parent and verbally interrupts, insisting on attention, is because he is not sure you know he is there. He is attempting to make his presence known. The little squeeze affirms awareness of his presence.

Teaching a child the appropriate way to interrupt your conversation with a third party is a gesture of honor and respect. It also demonstrates that love is kind and love is patient. Here are some benefits of the interrupt courtesy:

- It becomes a means for the child to give honor to others while at the same time communicating his need to the parent.

- The child learns to trust that the parent will meet his needs in an orderly way.

- It helps the child to grow in the discipline of patience.

- It reinforces the positive side of the child's conscience. Confirmation comes from within the heart of the child as well as from without.

- It communicates to the third party involved the standards of respect and honor by which you as a family are living.

Review your general parenting practice. If your son or daughter has never had to wait for anything, then waiting to interrupt properly will be difficult. Therefore, work on waiting at other times. For example, when the Ezzos' toddler grandchildren get out of the car in a parking lot of a grocery store, they hear from a supervising adult, "Hands on the car." This allows mom or dad time to gather up the baby without wondering where the siblings have wandered off to. Here, waiting is a health and safety issue, and it helps facilitate another virtue—patience.

Shyness and Respect

"But she's shy," blurted a mother apologetically. While shyness itself is not morally right or wrong, it does have moral facets. Shyness is not an acceptable excuse for disrespect. It cannot be used as a legitimate excuse for disrespect, because temperamental strengths and weaknesses do not exempt a child from right moral responses. If someone says hi to your child, the correct response should be, at the least, hi. If someone compliments your daughter's dress, teach her the basic courtesy response: "Thank you."

Train your children to be courteous. Before you leave for a social gathering, inform your children of the probability of receiving a compliment on their hair, clothing, or new shoes. Instruct them by teaching them how to rightly respond and, if necessary, inform them of the consequence if they fail to respond appropriately.

Yet you will have those moments. There you are, a good *Childwise* parent, full of moral intent and courtesy, staring at your child who just received a compliment. Out of his mouth comes…nothing. What do you do? First, don't make an excuse for the child. "Oh, he must be tired. He was up late last night." "I think he's getting sick." "He's shy like his dad." There is a better way. Simply smile at the person paying the delightful compliment and say, "I'm sorry, we are working on this." That's all.

There is no need to verbally dress down the child in public. It will not help for your child to see you display in public your frustration. Often parents pick that moment for a public battle. Nine times out of ten, it is the wrong moment. Wait until you get home to work through the consequences and the associated teaching.

A child's failure to respond appropriately is not as much a reflection on his or her temperament as it is on the parent's conviction and resolve to honor age. Respecting age is one of those nonnegotiable values that needs to be in the heart of every child.

Whatever Happened to Mr. and Mrs.?

Such titles, along with a host of endearing terms, got lost in your parents' generation. Here is a good place to rebel against the culture. Join the growing movement of those returning to the use of "Mr." and "Mrs."

Titles such as Mr. and Mrs., or when appropriate, sir and ma'am, and terms of endearment such as mom, dad, grandpa, grandma, aunt, and uncle are morally appropriate. Respecting age in these ways is not old-fashioned or out of vogue. Insist upon these actions in your children and teach the principles behind them. The effort will help in the process of cultivating right actions and beliefs in your child.

When a child applies the titles of Mr. and Mrs., he acknowledges that he is not the adult's equal. Although equal in a court of law and before the court of heaven, they are not equal in societal responsibility. The use of the titles Mr. and Mrs. is the child's acknowledgment that he is still young and in need of wisdom and life's experiences. He is still growing intellectually and needs the benefits offered by the elder population. Those reasons are legitimate and virtuous ones for honoring age.

"Calling me by my last name will make me feel old." Do you think that? Catch up with yourself. To the children in your world—surprise!—you *are* old. Others will say, "But I just want to be a friend to the child." Come on. Young children are more apt to develop contempt than friendship for adults they don't show respect for. Calling an adult by his or her first name is not going to make a child feel any closer to that adult.

The depth of relationship with any child is measured by the basics of relationship—kindness, patience, gentleness, a legitimate interest in what they say, respect, and much more. Not one of these attributes is encouraged by the absence of titles. How we act toward that child, not what we let them call us, determines the quality of our relationship with them. The titles Mr. and Mrs. simply provide a vehicle for children to honor and respect age.

Respect and honor are action words. That means that having an *attitude* of respect but without *action* does not go far enough. If attitude were enough, why make a child say, "I'm sorry"? The attitude of sorrow should be enough. Why insist that she say, "Thank you"? A thankful attitude should be enough. If an attitude of wanting to make something right is enough, it would absolve us of having to teach children to pay back something they have taken or broken.

Clearly, attitude is not enough; it must lead to action and application. Trying to teach your child an attitude of respect without providing a vehicle to demonstrate it engenders exasperation instead. "Mr." and "Mrs." are wonderful ways to respect age.

PEERS AND SIBLINGS

When Cara forgot her quarter for pretzel day at school, she sobbed all the way home. How she wanted to join her friends in purchasing that treat. But Cara learned a lesson that day. She gained great sympathy for any peer who likewise got left out. Next time, she was ready. She had a quarter for her own pretzel—and another for someone else, just in case. Sure enough, when pretzel day came around again, Cara's friend Stacy forgot to bring money. Instead of two pretzels for Cara, there was pretzel money for her empty-handed friend.

Teaching your child to respond in a sensitive way toward the feelings of his peers is a far greater act than just getting him to control his hostile behavior. Yes, hitting, pushing, and the little scrapes our children get into during the growing years have to be curbed. But these are not as much of a concern as developing a genuine empathy—sensitivity to the feelings of others. Respect for peers means more than restraining the dark side of a child's nature. It also means reaching out to others in times of need.

How can you teach respect, honor, and honesty? Work positively with your children and their relationship with siblings and friends. This starts at home.

Siblings: Conflict to Conflict

When we consider the various brothers and sisters mentioned in the corridors of history, we might draw the conclusion that conflict between siblings is legitimate. Cain and Abel, Jacob and Esau, and Joseph and his brothers are a few examples of sibling problems covered in the Bible. From the earliest days of human history, siblings have squabbled, endangering one of life's most precious relationships.

Sibling conflict is different from sibling rivalry. Rivalry takes place when a child perceives he is not loved, or loved as much, or in danger of losing parental love. First, he may act *out* to gain his parents' attention. If that does not work, he will act *up* against his parents.

Sibling conflict is not simply a phase that children go through. It is a moral problem that desperately needs correcting. Although sibling conflict is frustrating for any parent to observe, it is possible to carry out the first principle between siblings, but it will take consistent hard work. Here are a few suggestions to help you on the path to a more harmonious family.

Do not be satisfied with siblings who just tolerate each other. Instead, aim for the higher standard of sacrificial love. We have found that the way a child treats his siblings is often the way he will treat his future spouse and children. Do not curse your future grandchildren by not encouraging sufficient love between brothers and sisters now.

Teach your children how to resolve their own conflicts. The Ezzo and Bucknam children learned very early that sometimes, peaceably resolving their own conflicts is better than having dad come and resolve them. Usually neither side gets what it wanted.

Make a rule: No tattling. There is an old proverb that reminds us: The first to present his case seems right, till another comes forward and questions him.[7]

Children bring reports to their parents about siblings for many reasons; some are legitimate, and others are not. The legitimate reasons include health and safety concerns or the honest desire for parental intervention and justice. With the latter, the child has learned that sometimes it's better to consult a neutral mediator rather than escalate the conflict (by striking back at a sibling).

Actual tattling is when a brother or sister snitches for the sole purpose of getting another sibling in trouble. This is malice; the desire to see others receive pain. In the hierarchy of childhood crimes, this may be one of the worst offenses. Often, it is done in hopes of gaining both parental approval and assistance—approval for not being the one doing wrong, and assistance in gaining the upper hand on his sibling by bringing the matter to his parents' attention.

In the Ezzo and Bucknam homes, the tattler received the consequence they had hoped would fall on the sibling. Our children knew the difference between coming to us with a legitimate concern and coming to get a sibling in trouble. Humility and concern, not malice, was what prompted one sibling to report on another. Even then they could not come unless they had first tried to get their sibling to stop whatever he or she was doing wrong before coming to us. It works well.

Require verbal and physical kindness between siblings. Teach verbal and physical self-control. Give your children guidance in relation to their treatment of siblings and friends. These boundaries include restrictions on hitting, pushing, talking back, and a general lack of self-control. Take advantage of family times (such as at the dinner table or driving in the car) to model this. Take turns sharing what each one appreciates about another member of the family.

One commonsense rule is for children to keep their hands to themselves. If a sibling gets hit, rather than striking back, he must have the confidence to know that his parents will bring justice. The door of escape is not retaliation, but seeking out the one in charge, whether it be mom at home or a teacher on the playground. Justice comes from rightly exercised authority.

You have heard it said, "If you don't have something nice to say, don't say anything at all." Your children should never speak rudely to each other. Evil intended remarks such as, "I don't love you," "You're ugly," or threats like, "I'm going to tell," are unacceptable. Keep watch! Training children to restrain their unkind speech is one of the most overlooked areas in parenting.

Teach your children how to respect each other. The following areas of training are often overlooked:

- listening attentively to a brother or a sister;
- responding with the basic courtesies and greetings such as, "Please," "Thank you," "Goodnight," "I'm sorry," or, "Will you forgive me?";
- interrupting properly, with only one person speaking at a time;
- sharing property that is reasonable to share;
- being genuinely happy when something good happens to a sibling.

Encourage your children to be happy when something wonderful happens to a sibling or friend, such as when one receives an award, wins at a board game, or has an opportunity that the others do not have. Your constant encouragement in this area can make the difference between ongoing bickering between siblings and a peaceful home.

Another way this is realized is at a sibling's birthday. You do not need to buy a gift for everyone attending the child's party. That only robs the birthday child of his special day. It teaches the siblings to selfishly look forward to a day of gifts rather than a day of giving, celebrating the birth of a brother or sister.

Mothers will often say, "I don't want anyone to feel bad because he didn't get a gift." But they *will* all receive a gift—each one on his own birthday. And if someone feels bad that he didn't get a gift, that only tells you where that child needs some work—the virtue of contentment.

Provide an environment that will encourage service to others. Take household chores, for example. Researchers from Toronto, Canada, and from Macquarie University in Australia studied children from families who were given daily chores and those who were not. Their research pointed toward some interesting conclusions.

Children who performed household chores showed more compassion for their siblings and other family members than children who did not share in family responsibility. Even more interesting was the fact that not all chores were considered equal. The kids who did family-care chores, like setting the table, feeding the cat, or bringing in firewood, showed more concern for the welfare of others than children who had only self-care responsibilities, such as making their own bed and hanging up their own clothes.

Whenever children participate in the care of others, they grow sensitive to human need. Include your children in helping to secure the welfare of your family. That may mean bringing in firewood every day after school, helping out with weeding the garden, or setting or clearing the table. Whatever it may look like in your home, include your children in the experience of daily serving others. Their joy in doing so may surprise you.

SUMMARY

How sensitive is your child toward others? That question takes us right back to our first principle: love your neighbor as yourself; other people count. When your child's neighbor is thirsty, will your child offer him a drink? When your child's neighbor is hungry, will he ask to take him some food? When your child's neighbor is cold, will he think of a way to help? When your child's neighbor is alone, will he reach out in friendship?

To have your son or daughter reach out to another child for no other reason than love makes it all worthwhile. Children whose hearts are inclined to others are a blessing—and not just to other people, but to the parents as well. They are vessels of mercy to those who know no mercy and grace to those who know no grace. Is that your child?

Morally trained children know how to respect property, age, and peers. Such children are a joy to be around, because they are complete, equipped with moral reason. They are not the product of chance or genetics. People will mistakenly say to these parents, "You're so lucky to have children like that." But it's not luck, it's the result of consistent, persistent, parental training. These children's actions demonstrate humility of heart, which is what real character training is all about.

QUESTIONS FOR REVIEW

1. Explain the impact or value of any commodity? Explain your answer.

2. Summarize the purpose of the interrupt courtesy.

3. What is meant by the statement, "Not all chores are equal"?

SECTION THREE

DISCIPLINE

Chapter Seven

At the Heart of Discipline

Six-year-old Tommy is having a field day terrorizing the swim club toddler pool with his new super-soaker water gun. Moments later, mom comes onto the scene. "Tommy, give it to me. Tom, give me the gun. Tommy, don't you point that at…Tommyyyyy, don't YOU DARRRRE!"

Too late. Mom finally disarms little Tommy, but she's soaked. Cute, huh? Losing the squirter is no big loss for Tommy. There's still fifty ways to stir up trouble, all stored in his struggling heart. Such slices of life are common today.

Here's another. Imagine for a moment that after picking up your first-grader at school, you decide to stop at a local ice cream shop for a special treat. You step up to the counter and order two hot fudge sundaes with nuts. Moments later, you sit down at the table together. Your child smiles innocently at you, then buries her nose in the chocolate topping.

"Stop that!" But your words have no effect. Your precious little girl's fingers dig into the ice cream like miniature shovels. Within moments, the table is a sticky mess. "Don't!" you protest again, more quietly this time.

You want your child to end this embarrassing behavior, but you are unwilling to put any muscle behind your command. You decide to watch and hold your tongue. Maybe there's no need to step in. Surely she will outgrow this behavior.

The cliché "children will be children" is true. Children *will* be children. That's why parents need to be parents. No child is endowed with self-control from birth. No three-year-old has experienced enough in life to know how to govern his own behavior without guidance from caretakers. Parents fulfill the role of teachers and mentors. How they can motivate children to do the right things and shun the wrong is the topic of section 3. We're going to talk about discipline.

WHAT IS IT?

A child who disobeys may hear his mother say, "I'm afraid I'm going to have to discipline you for that." This is a common, but misused, application of the word *discipline*. Today, we define discipline as punishment. But discipline in its truest sense refers to one thing: training. Heart training.

Discipline is a process of training that encourages consistent behavior. It keeps children on track, and sometimes puts them back on track. The word *discipline* comes from the same Latin root (*discipulus*) as "disciple"—one who is a learner. Parents are the teachers, children are the disciples.

Disciplining—heart training—is best accomplished by parenting from the first principle. Values-based discipline urges children to treat other people the way they want to be treated. Neither child-centered nor authoritarian parenting styles emphasize personal responsibility, inner growth, self-control, and other virtues the way first principle parenting does.

We have found that if parents shape their child's heart and character, they will not have to concentrate as much on reshaping the child's outward behavior.

HOW WILL THEY KNOW?

There is an old Jewish proverb that states: "Discipline your son, and he will give you peace; he will bring delight to your soul."[8] In this context, the word *discipline* means to educate your child. It doesn't mean to punish but to train. As you do, both peace and delight are your rewards. The message is clear: In order for your child to learn, your job as a parent is to teach.

CHILDWISE PRINCIPLE #9
Discipline is heart food for your child.

How you communicate instruction is at least as important as the instruction itself. It's as essential for the development of proper discipline as healthy food is to physical development. Instruction is the starting point of all moral training. In the stories at the beginning of this chapter, both mothers thought they were instructing their children. They weren't. They were merely reacting to a situation already out of control.

As a parent, listen to the type of instruction you give. Are you the type who only gives commands? Or do you tend to give suggestions hoping for compliance? Do your instructions teach to the intellect but not the heart? Do you demand a new task of your child without demonstrating how it is accomplished? Do you instruct more with words of restraint than with words of encouragement?

Tip #1: Accentuate the Positive

In chapter 5, we discussed how parents typically spend more time and energy suppressing wayward behavior in their children than elevating good behavior. While words of restraint are necessary throughout the training process, we must retool ourselves to communicate the positive.

When communicating with your children, attempt to speak as often as possible in the positive, not the negative. If there is something you don't want your child to do, then communicate your desire for restraint by speaking in favor of what you want done. Here is a sample list to help you get in the habit of positive speech.

Instead of this:	Consider this:
"Don't spill your cereal."	"See how carefully you can carry your cereal bowl."
"Don't get out of bed."	"Obey Mommy and stay in bed."
"Don't hit your sister."	"You need to show kindness to your sister."

Instead of this:	Consider this:
"Don't talk so much."	"You need to learn to become a good listener."
"Don't chew with your mouth open."	"Chew quietly with your mouth closed."
"Don't leave a mess for everyone else to clean up."	"Be responsible and clean up after yourself."

With young children, there will be plenty of justifiable *don'ts:* "Don't touch the knives," "Don't play with the stereo," "Don't hit the dog." Such prohibitions are appropriate and necessary. But as your child grows, you should make a transition so that positive instruction becomes the norm.

Most methods of instruction have value, and there is a time and a place for almost all of them, but they are usually most effective during periods of nonconflict. Unfortunately, what usually happens is that we communicate moral truth predominately in times of conflict, when correcting a misbehavior. Your daughter takes a toy from another child. You step in with correction to fix the problem. You explain the moral wrongness of the act, hoping the child will learn the lesson in the moment.

Our point is this: If all of your moral instruction is given during periods of conflict, when teaching restraint, then the pathway to virtuous living will be missed. You've told them what not to do, but not what *to* do. Those times of nonconflict are best for parents to accentuate the positive.

Tip #2: Substitution, Not Just Suppression

The Ezzos were once approached by a father asking how to deal with his son's obsessive jealousy. That question leads to a broader one: How do you correct not just jealousy, but all attitudes of the heart? How do you help your child overcome attitudes like envy, revenge, and spitefulness?

Children of all ages are better served by *substitution* than by *suppression*. The father mentioned above was frustrated by his efforts to suppress his son's jealousy. No matter how hard he tried to keep the lid on it, jealousy continued to leak out. The problem here and for many parents is not simply the presence of a vice but the absence of a virtue. The strategy then is to equally increase the child's awareness to what is right and what he should be doing. Identify the vice and then work on the opposite virtue.

Suppression of wrong behavior is often achieved by encouraging the opposite virtue. If you want to suppress jealousy, give equal time to elevating the opposite virtue: contentment. If you have a child struggling with envy, teach charity. For anger, teach self-control. For revenge, teach forgiveness. Substitution will make all the difference in the world. Our young father above did just that. It wasn't easy, and it didn't happen overnight, but his son's jealousy was mastered when he learned contentment.

What does it look like in your home? Children learn by the words we say. Instruction is a real part of the heart training process. But in the average home most of our instructions come during moments of greatest frustration. Learning how to give instructions in such a way that your child will obey, without either one of you being exasperated, is a worthy pursuit.

Sooner or later, every parent must decide what obedience will look like in his or her home. The definition is not usually forged out of a mental exercise with pen and paper but from the reality of what happens after giving instruction. For some parents, obedience means prompt response, without murmuring or complaining. For others it means anything but that. Some parents count 1-2-3. Others counts "8-9-9 1/2-9 3/4...I mean it, I'll say 10..." Whatever it looks like in your home, try to improve upon it.

Believe it or not, it is possible to give instruction and receive back a prompt, courteous response. And you can accomplish this without shouting, chasing after, or threatening the child with loss of limb, liberty, or lollipops.

Tip #3: How Many Times Will You Say "Now"?

"Blake," she called. "BLake...BLAke...BLAKe...BLAKE! COME HERE! Blake, I'm not telling you again. Get over here. NOW Blake! I mean it! Blake...!"

Look familiar? The mother or father who first coaxes, then threatens, then bargains, then pretends to punish, then finally punishes (a little) is only making a bad situation worse. Why should a child ever respond the first time if he knows he'll get twenty-six more chances, at the end of which there is no penalty and often is a reward?

Airports are such great places for parenting educators like us. We see it all in the terminals. The most common sight? The repeated command, followed by threats—threats that parents are counting on to intimidate the little Blakes of the world into compliance. "Blake, I am going to get on the plane without you." Such tactics usually backfire. In this actual case, Blake, who could not have been more than four years old, told his mom, "Have a nice trip."

Who's got the problem? Obviously not Blake. He is doing exactly what he wants. Why does Blake tune mom out and probably dad as well? He has discovered that, in his little world, obedience is optional.

This mom and dad suffer from the repeating threat syndrome. All guilty of same raise your right hand. We all sometimes fall into the threatening/repeating trap, including the authors of this book. But the issue is not whether we are guilty from time to time, but whether we are characterized by a pattern of such poor instruction. Is that how we almost always try to parent? When parents lack resolve behind their instructions, children lack the motivation to comply, and parents are too often left begging.

Even the most habitual threat-repeating mom and dad will finally get to the breaking point. The child recognizes all the signals: high blood pressure, red face, increased voice intensity, a mother incoherently talking to herself or possessed with a glazed homicidal—or suicidal—look. That is when the child knows, obey now or die.

Why get to that point? May we suggest that you *never give an instruction unless you intend for it to be obeyed*. Say what you mean and mean what you say.

Here is a bit of encouraging news for parents. Your children will not have a problem with this principle. Usually it is only mom and dad who struggle with it, because it calls parents to consistency. Children will rise to whatever level of parental resolve is present. How much determination lies behind your instructions?

Tip #4: Provide a Five-Minute Warning

Sometimes the timing of instruction is as important as the instruction itself. We have all gotten completely absorbed in a project, so we know how frustrating it is when we are forced to leave our efforts without warning. The same frustration is felt by children. There are times when it is appropriate to provide a five-minute warning that a call for compliance will soon follow. Such a benevolent act helps any child emotionally prepare to comply.

Kyle, Stevie, and Rachel marched their little game pieces around the board. Their mother interrupted and informed them that in five minutes she would return with instructions for them to prepare the dinner table. That five-minute warning made obedience more attractive for the kids. They were able to psychologically prepare for the game to be suspended, rather than being yanked away mid-hop.

Such parental sensitivity reduces the shock of intrusion and alleviates the tension between the child's desire to continue with his activity and the need to comply with his mother's instruction. A five-minute warning helps children emotionally prepare to yield to your instructions.

What happens if the parent gives instructions but the child continues his activity beyond the five minutes? James was watching a favorite cartoon when mom alerted him with a five-minute warning. Five minutes later, mom's instruction came, but James did not move. He watched the next cartoon and the next. He sat to the end of the program, then to the next commercial, and into the next program.

James's behavior was plainly disobedience. He decided to accept his own preference instead of his mother's instruction and then took advantage of her graciousness. Mom's contribution to this behavior was not following up. She had no resolve to have her instructions followed. Some might think it is a minor thing that the child stretched his time. But open defiance is not a little fault, and the judicial parent should not turn her back on this attitude. It will only become a way of life. How can James's behavior be curbed?

Tip #5: Require a "Yes, Mom" or "Yes, Dad" Response

Of all the practical helps we can offer, this one has undoubtedly the most impact on a child's willingness and ability to comply *the first time.*

Require your children to respond to your instructions with a "Yes, mom" or "Yes, dad." Such a response does not leave you second-guessing. You do not have to ask repeatedly, "Did you hear me?" which only undermines your leadership. Upon saying, "James, in five minutes Mom is going to ask you to put away your puzzle." Mom should hear back, "Yes, Mom."

Why a verbal response? Number one, it is the child's acknowledgment that in fact he heard you. A "Yes, mom" lets you know that your child is either committing himself to obedience by taking the appropriate action or to disobedience by avoiding the task asked of him. But there's no question that he heard.

How does a verbal response produce obedience? A parent's initial instruction draws a line in the sand. "Honey, Mom wants you to pick up your crayons right now, please." She should stick with that. If she repeats her instruction, she draws a second line in the sand. It is a small retreat. "Did you hear me? Pick up your crayons." Another repeat is yet a greater retreat. Soon, mom's on the floor either begging the child or picking up crayons.

But in contrast, when your child gives back to you a "Yes, mom," an amazing thing happens. Your child hears himself commit to obey. He draws the line in the sand himself. There's just something about hearing himself agree to something that elicits an internal compulsion for compliance.

"Yes, mom" or "Yes, dad" stops conflict at the point of instructions. Parents experience more frustration at times of instruction than in any other single activity in parenting. Why? Because it is at this point that children decide to obey or disobey. Disobedience brings conflict, and usually the repeating parent comes out losing. Once repeating starts, obedience is lost and frustration wells up. And that is with just one child.

The antidote? Never get out of the instruction phase without an agreement to obey. An up-front "Yes, mom" virtually eliminates the problem.

Some instruction will be very specific, especially with two, three, and four-year-olds. "Bradon," one mother called out, "do not play with the bird food. Say, 'Yes, Mommy.'" Bradon's two-year-old hands were wrist deep in the sunflower mix. If mom had only given the instruction: "Bradon, stop playing with the bird food," his little hands would still be sifting seed today. But because of the "Yes, mom" training, he replied and then drew his little fingers out of the bag. Is this simply a little boy with incredible self-control? No, it is a developmental dynamic associated with a verbal "Yes, Mommy" response.

You know that moment immediately after the point of instruction, when you can see a question in your little guy's eyes: *"Hmm, do I really want to obey this woman—right now?"* Now you don't have to hold your breath wondering if he's going to comply or not. In that moment, you only need to say, "Bradon, I need to hear 'Yes, Mommy.'" His response moves him beyond the moment of a wrong decision.

Let's go back to the five-minute warning. Mom enters the room while a board game is well in progress. "Stevie, Kyle, Rachel, Mom is giving you a five-minute warning. In five minutes you will need to stop your game and get ready for dinner." Now is when mom should hear back: "Yes, Mom." Bingo. The children have just given mom their confirmation to commit to her instructions.

Initially, if you have a child that is used to ignoring you, you might have to hold her little face up to you while giving instruction. Make it a standard practice to get your child to look you in the eyes when speaking. Eye contact is a focusing skill and helps any child process instruction, and processing instruction is half the battle in getting a child to follow through promptly. The child that looks around the room rather than at mom or dad when receiving instruction tends to struggle more with compliance.

How to begin. When introducing this "Yes, mom" and "Yes, dad" concept, start by sitting the family down and explaining what will be required. You can even make a game of it.

A father told us that one afternoon he sat down with his four-year-old daughter to have this talk. He instructed her to first listen for dad's voice, and then upon hearing him call her name, she was to say, "Yes, Daddy," and immediately come to him. In return she got a big hug from dad. Over the course of that afternoon and evening, he played this little game twenty times and she responded twenty times with a "Yes, Daddy." That evening, when tucking the child in bed, he told her, "Starting tomorrow, whenever Mom or Dad calls, you're to say, 'Yes, Mom' or 'Yes, Dad' and come immediately, like we played today."

This little exercise has worked with many families. What makes it work is the resolve behind the parents' instruction.

One side note. If children are going to respond to parents in kindness, parents should do the same for their children. If we are truly governed by the first principle, then we will treat others (including our children) the way we want to be treated.

Recently, one of the Ezzo grandchildren paid a visit. After finishing some schoolwork, Ashley called her grandmother. "Grammy?" Anne Marie answered, "Yes, Ashley." For children, a "Yes, Mom" is a *moral requirement*. That is because they are in the process of becoming moral. For adults, "Yes, Ashley," is a *moral courtesy*, given by one who has reached maturity.

When your children call you, do you answer, "What do you want?" Or do they receive a courteous reply? Kindness is never outgrown.

SUMMARY

Learning how to effectively communicate instructions to our children is essential to proper parenting—and to avoiding problems. Many parent/child conflicts start here. And remember, once in a while we may repeat ourselves. Sometimes repeating may be legitimate and other times it may not be. However, we should be working toward a pattern of consistency without resorting to repetition. Someday, a first-time response may save your child's life. You can train your child to tune you in rather than tune you out.

QUESTIONS FOR REVIEW

1. What is discipline?

2. How is discipline different from punishment?

3. What do the authors mean when they advise parents to accentuate the positive?

4. Explain the concept of substitution versus suppression.

5. What does a five-minute warning do for a child?

6. Why is it so important to get a "Yes, Mom" response after giving instruction?

Chapter Eight

Five Laws of Correction

*T*wo four-year-old cousins were striking the dwarf plum tree with sturdy sticks. Laughing and chanting a nursery rhyme, the pair used their enchanted scepters to knock from the branches the newly formed plums. Too late, grandma discovered and stopped their fairy-tale game. Previously, spring rains had wiped out all but a couple dozen plums. Now, nearly half of those lay on the ground.

Maybe you don't have plum trees, but chances are you have a child whose curiosity or mischievousness will lead him to commit an unwelcome deed. Let's face it: life is full of temptations. Have hose, will squirt. Have pretty flowers, will pick. Have quiet space, will scream. Have time to sit, will move. There's no doubt that young lives require training. That is the reason we discipline our children. They must learn to live safely, wisely, and in a manner respectful of those around them.

Part of this guidance comes from encouraging right behavior, and part comes by correction. In this chapter, we will limit our discussion to the corrective side of parental guidance. Later chapters will deal with the encouragement side. *Correction* means to bring back from error, or to align an unacceptable deviation back to the standard. While parental encouragement keeps children on track and moving forward, correction is used to get them back on track.

The correction side of discipline is guided by certain fixed principles. These are the fundamentals of correction, the filter through which all corrections must pass. If you and your spouse are operating out of these same principles, you will usually be able to come to the same disciplining conclusions without needing a time-out huddle or cell phone emergency call each time your child crosses the line. This is good news. Not only is the phone bill slashed in half but your child gets consistent consequences no matter which parent is doing the correcting.

Our aim in this chapter is to provide a way for any parent, in any discipline situation, to administer correction fairly and effectively. This can be done by consistently employing five laws of correction.

FIRST LAW OF CORRECTION:
DISTINGUISH BETWEEN CHILDISHNESS AND DEFIANCE

You are completely humiliated. Little Jenny delights in poking her head under the bathroom stall to see who's inside. Last time there was no one so you didn't fuss. This time, however, she intrudes on a handicapped woman. Suddenly, it's a major violation and you wish you had stopped this game long before now.

Where is the line between innocent play and malicious behavior? When does curiosity cross the line to snooping? At what point does a misdemeanor become a felony? When do wrong actions become malicious disobedience?

If parenting were all about drawing lines, we would quickly run out of chalk. Fortunately, a thick black line has already been drawn for us in permanent ink. It marks the border between two totally separate realms of behavior. On one side is the land of Childish Mistakes. On the other is the land of Defiant Misdeeds. While the two nations have similar names, the difference between them is profound. The first speaks of nonrebellious acts, the second speaks of acts committed with malicious intent. Both require correction, but of different kinds.

There is a distinction between the child who accidentally hurts his brother while playing, and the child who does so with the intention of inflicting pain. There is a difference between the child who accidentally damages property and the one who intentionally vandalizes. And there is a difference between bumping into a dwarf plum tree by accident and striking it with sticks to make the fruit fall to the ground.

The Ezzos have another fruit tree, this one a semi-dwarf grapefruit tree. It bears fruit once a year. In terms of size and color, the grapefruit look mature in November. However, they do not fully ripen until February and March. One Thanksgiving weekend, a group of three- and four-year-olds were playing in the back yard. One child saw all the yellow grapefruit and thought he would help Mr. Ezzo by picking them. After all, last week he had helped his uncle harvest grapefruit (which came from a year-round producing tree), so he knew all about it. All the children joined in and picked a half-bushel of unripe grapefruit.

The children had no knowledge regarding the ripening process of dwarf grapefruit. It was the lack of knowledge, not a malicious intent of the heart, that drove their behavior. In fact, their intent was noble—to help Mr. Ezzo. Their actions were simply childish. What they did was wrong, but they didn't do it to be wrong. That afternoon, they received a lecture from their parents about touching even ripe-looking fruit on trees without asking permission.

Let's look at the words *childishness* and *defiance*. We use the term *childishness* to refer to innocent immaturity. This includes those nonmalicious, nonrebellious, accidental mistakes our children make, such as spilling a glass of water, accidentally bumping another person, or picking fruit from a neighbor's tree as in the case above. Childishness is when a child does something wrong but wouldn't have if she'd been able to prevent it (accidents) or had known it was wrong. *Defiance,* on the other hand, implies bad motives. The child knew the act was wrong, but did it anyway.

Childishness is usually a *head* problem—a lack of knowledge. Defiance is usually a *heart* problem—the child does not want to do right.

Nine-year-old Nate sneaked into the house looking for a good hiding place. Going from corner to corner with childhood glee, his foot caught a wire and a porcelain lamp crashed to the floor. Promptly, all the children were gathered together and told that the inside of the house was off-limits for hide-and-seek. With nods of understanding, they all went back outside. Twenty minutes later, Nate's six-year-old sister, Nicole, came sneaking into the house looking for a place to hide.

Now, Nicole did exactly what her brother did, right? Nate had entered the house playing hide-and-seek, and so had she. But there's a huge difference. Nate did it in childish innocence. Nicole did it with full knowledge of her wrong. She did it in defiance of her parents' instruction.

Motive is what separates childishness from defiance. When instructions have been given and received about something, there is little room for "innocent mistakes" regarding that behavior. If the wrong thing is intentionally done, it's disobedience—outright defiance—pure and simple.

Parents should correct both childishness and defiance. But the form of correction will differ. When assessing a behavior in need of correction, parents should ask themselves, "Was my child's action the result of an accident, a misunderstanding, a lack of knowledge—or purposeful defiance or intent to cause harm?" How that question is answered will determine what happens next.

THE SECOND LAW OF CORRECTION:
ALL CORRECTION MUST PROMOTE LEARNING

"Becky, don't splash your baby sister in the face," mom says, only to see her Becky wander across the wading pool to her next victim. Splash. Splash. Mom is shocked and the shouting ensues. If only mom had explained the real issue behind Becky's first playful flick of water.

CHILDWISE PRINCIPLE #10
If learning didn't take place, correction didn't happen.

Correction requires explanation. Without the why of wrong there is no correction, just a random redirection of behavior. Whether a child's actions be innocent mistakes or malicious disobedience, explanatory teaching will always be necessary. The parent's job is to move the child from what he did this time to what he should do next time. Whatever the wrong, use it to impart knowledge. If you complete your talk and learning didn't take place, correction didn't happen.

Don't be fooled. The reason five young children never picked unripened grapefruit again was not because they were severely punished (they weren't), but because they were made to understand why their actions were wrong. Knowledge that they formerly did not have became the basis of their future self-restraint. Meaningful correction took place.

Children learn by gaining knowledge but not all knowledge comes through textbooks or living room lectures. Sometimes we teach our kids what not to do by walking them through behaviors.

In the Ezzos' vegetable garden there is a series of brick walkways which children thrill in playfully weaving through. Sometimes, however, little two-year-old feet mindlessly leave the path. A toddler has no knowledge of the plants underfoot. She would not understand a discourse on the recovery rate of crushed cucumber stems. Education in this case is facilitated by hands-on learning—taking the child for a walk on the bricks, pointing out where she can step and where she cannot. Make the education you give age-appropriate. Just be sure to give it.

Children learn in a variety of ways. Sometimes the painful consequences associated with their actions become their tutors. Let's say your child ignores your instructions to not exit the swing in midair. His beautiful brush burn on his right thigh is the natural consequence. It teaches him the *why* behind your prohibition.

Consider the behavioral explanation you give today to be a deposit on tomorrow's behavior. Your goal is to transfer the impetus for right moral behavior from the external (you) to the internal (your child). That cannot happen without the why of behavior.

THE THIRD LAW OF CORRECTION:
MAKE THE PUNISHMENT FIT THE CRIME

It's natural for parents to react spontaneously to negative behavior. You see defiance and boom, you jump on it. But before you jump, stop and think. You must act for the child's good. Recklessly reacting in the heat of the moment isn't the best plan.

In the past, the Ezzos once attended a church whose pastor's solution for misbehaving children was simple. "Parenting is not all that difficult," he repeatedly proclaimed from his pulpit. "If your child disobeys, beat him." We would like to report that this was said in jest, but he was deadly serious. Beating children is not a solution for parenting nor an acceptable form of responsible punishment. Offering such simple solutions misdirects parents and robs them of any incentive to think, evaluate, and assess the context of a child's actions, his age, or the commonness of his offense.

Where should parents begin when considering correction for their children's intentional disobedience? Disobedient behavior needs correction, but parents should not correct all disobedience the same way or with the same strength of consequence. Parents should modify their correction based on the following five factors.

The age of the child. Am I training a toddler who is just learning to put his world together or a second-grader approaching the middle years of childhood?

The frequency of the offense. Is this the first time this offense has been committed in six months or the sixth time in six minutes? Correction should be handled with reference to frequency. If the first offense was handled at correction level one (whatever that may be in your home), the second, third, and sixteenth occurrences should be treated at progressively higher correction levels.

The context of the moment. Context is not an excuse for disobedience, but it should be taken into consideration when determining consequences. Look back to the original inciting incident to determine context. Did your child disobey as part of the group, or was he the leader of the insurrection?

The overall characterization of behavior. Is this the only behavior in need of correction or is it part of a larger pattern in need of attention? Is this the kind of thing your child often does or was it some strange aberration? Is there some deeper problem that's causing this behavior? Perhaps you would be wasting effort treating a symptom.

The need for balance. When considering consequences, parents should also consider that overly harsh punishment exasperates a child, while excessive leniency fails to put a correct value on the offense. You know your child. Decide what level of punitive effect is appropriate for the offense and take action that is calculated to achieve that effect.

THE FOURTH LAW OF CORRECTION: AN OFFENSE AGAINST A PERSON OR PROPERTY REQUIRES AN APOLOGY

This law of correction is completely incompatible with child-centered parenting. A child's moral sensibility is intimately connected to his or her willingness to accept responsibility for wrongful actions. This awareness cannot be a silent introspection. Teach your children to admit they're wrong when they're wrong. It is the first step in mending wounds.

Relationships work best when there is no unresolved conflict simmering within them. That is why this fourth law is so much a part of healthy families. Have you ever been offended by a friend, coworker, or family member and the person knows he's done wrong but refuses to admit it? At best, he'll just be unusually nice to you for a while. That's his way of apologizing without having to admit wrong. But it's unsatisfactory.

You may not be able to change your coworkers, friends, father or mother, or brother or sister, but you can certainly train your children in this area. Think how these relationships bother you. Don't let it happen in your family between siblings or between your child and you.

Humility is the basis for healthy families. Seeking forgiveness for an offense and humbly admitting error in an effort to be restored with the offended party is a prerequisite for a loving and enduring relationship. This is serious heart business. Children and adults who are in the habit of asking for forgiveness take ownership of their wrong actions. They show they believe the relationship is worth the possible embarrassment often associated with admitting wrong.

In practice, what does an apology look like? What are the components? First, understand the distinction between saying "I'm sorry" and asking for forgiveness. Both are appropriate but not always in the same situations. "I'm sorry" is associated with unintentional mistakes, childishness. Apologizing expresses regret over an action that caused hurt but which was void of malice or hurtful intent. Seeking forgiveness on the other hand is appropriate when the person has willfully committed a hurtful act. There was intention to defy, injure, or destroy. This is a heart problem.

When Kenny unintentionally stepped in Mrs. Brown's flower bed and uprooted a couple of new plants, his mom had him apologize by saying, "I'm sorry, Mrs. Brown, for stepping on your flowers." That was an appropriate response since his actions were childish and devoid of purposeful wrongdoing. Kenny's "I'm sorry" does not signal guilt but his acknowledgment of the innocent wrong.

Let's change the scenario slightly and add a second dimension: instruction. We'll say Kenny had received instructions from Mrs. Brown not to play near the flower bed. He even received a second warning from his mother. But Kenny chose to ignore both, leading to the trampling of the flowers.

In this case, Kenny's actions just leaped from childishness to defiance. His actions can no longer be blamed on innocent immaturity. In the first instance, he did not know any better. This time around, he disregarded Mrs. Brown's instructions and continued on a careless path. Simply put, he disobeyed.

Here a simple "I'm sorry" isn't enough. Kenny is compelled to a deeper commitment: seeking forgiveness. "Mrs. Brown, will you forgive me for playing in the flower bed even though you told me not to?" A matter of semantics? Not at all. The difference is great. To say "I'm sorry" is to acknowledge a mistake; to ask for forgiveness is to acknowledge a bad motive of the heart. This is a humble acceptance of guilt. *Mea culpa!* (it was my fault).

Not convinced? Try it out on your marriage. The next time you and your spouse get to that place in a dispute where you are ready to make amends, seek out your spouse and, instead of just saying, "I'm sorry," say, "Honey, will you forgive me for losing control of my tongue?" or "Will you forgive me for being so stubborn?" Difficult? You bet. Try it a couple of times and you will realize its curbing power. You will find yourself guarding your tongue and actions more fervently. And that is exactly what happens with morally sensitive children.

Why is this forgiveness thing so powerful? Simply, it gets to the *heart* of the matter. Our hearts. When you say "I'm sorry," you're in control of that moment. You control the depth and sincerity of your sorrow. But when you seek forgiveness, the one you're humbling yourself before is in control. You're asking something of that person that you cannot get without his or her consent—forgiveness. It is this humbling effect that so wonderfully curbs a child's (and a parent's) appetite for going back and doing the same wrong thing again.

To train this into your child, guide her to the phrase, "Mom, I'm sorry," when she makes a mistake. When there is an act of defiance, teach her to ask forgiveness. "Sister, will you forgive me?" In both cases, have her add on a confession of the specific infraction. "Sister, will you forgive me for taking your toy?" Confession, as they say, is good for the soul.

This training will help cure your child of the "It was only an accident" sob story, which goes something like this. Mom says, "Honey, you need to say you're sorry to Mr. Franklin for knocking down all of the boxes."

"But Mom!" Adam says, "I didn't mean to do it. It was just an accident. I shouldn't have to say I'm sorry."

This condition is the result of only teaching apologies with the phrase "I'm sorry" and not "Will you forgive me?" When parents limit the options, they unintentionally force a child into unnecessary self-incrimination. If "I'm sorry" is linked to both innocent mistakes and purposeful wrong, then a child struggles with accepting responsibility for his honest mistakes.

In the scene above, the son could not say "I'm sorry" because he would be admitting guilt to something he did not intentionally do. That is why separating childishness from defiance necessitates the two forms of apology. It keeps "I'm sorry" where it belongs, in the category of mistakes. A child is more willing to accept responsibility for his childish mistakes if he knows that saying "I'm sorry" will not falsely incriminate him. "I'm sorry" means one thing. Seeking forgiveness, while more difficult, means quite another.

THE FIFTH LAW OF CORRECTION:
IF FINANCIAL LIABILITY OCCURS, THE CHILD
SHOULD HELP MAKE RESTITUTION

Restitution is defined as repayment for lost, damaged, or stolen property. The principle of restitution was very much part of American Judeo-Christian ethics forty years ago. If you broke a friend's cookie jar, you bought a new one and filled it with cookies. Homemade, even. If you uprooted the neighbor's plant, you replaced it with a healthy, larger, look-alike.

Whenever financial liability occurs, either as a result of mistakes or of intentional wrongdoing, restitution should be part of the restoration process. It is also a wonderful teacher. Parents should take financial responsibility for their child's behavior until he is old enough to take ownership of it himself. Along the way, the child can contribute—if not financially, then in some other community service-type activities to "make it right."

Some scholars are of the opinion that within ancient Hebrew culture, forgiveness was not complete until the offender made restitution. Restitution was the outward sign of one's desire to make amends. Jewish laws required restitution in cases of property damage or loss, whether intentional or unintentional.[9] We cite this historical point to demonstrate the antiquity of the concept. Restitution has been around a long time.

Restitution is not only a corrective concept but a disciplinary method—a consequence. The general rule is as follows: When injury is done as a result of childishness, restitution is one for one

(1:1). Destroy one flower, replace one flower. When injury is done as a result of willful defiance, then restitution should be 2:1, 3:1, or even 4:1, depending on parental judgment.[10]

Let's look at an example. "I bought a case of soft drinks for our upcoming family reunion," said one frustrated father. "Then I discovered that my ten- and twelve-year-old boys had helped themselves to a third of the cans. They knew that soda was for the reunion next Saturday. How do I punish them?"

The answer: restitution. Since this father had told his sons not to touch the soda and given the reason why, this was a sure case of defiance. Clearly they should be required to replace what they took, but, since it was a deliberate disobedience, the replacement rate should be higher than 1:1. We suggested that for every can taken, three cans were to be replaced.

The boys had to earn money by working around the house and neighborhood. This kind of restitution, by the way, reinforces to children the true value of a dollar. Their work satisfied both a training and restitution purpose. The father reported back to us: "It worked. The boys learned their lesson and the folks at the family reunion never had so much root beer!"

Restitution is a good teacher. It was effective in this case because of the boys' age. As we said, it also instills a basic understanding of the value of a dollar (this is usually best taught to children six years of age and higher). If the child does not have the means to repay, the parent then serves as his proxy and should make restitution to the injured party while teaching their actions to their child. Even three-year-olds can do work to make restitution:

help bake cookies, draw a picture expressing regret for the offense, or help Dad wash the offended party's car.

SUMMARY

Correction is not about getting even with your child, but about teaching. Heart training. The aim is to make the right path clear to your child and, when necessary, put him back on it. You correct for the specific purpose of bringing about change in the child's heart. Because a teachable, humble spirit is the goal of parenting.

QUESTIONS FOR REVIEW

We'd like to invite you to work through the following scenarios. The purpose of this exercise is to help you become familiar with each of the five laws of correction and the thought pattern necessary to bring fair and productive correction into your child's world. (You may wish to write on a separate sheet of paper.)

Scenario One

You come upon the scene described at the beginning of this chapter. Two four-year-olds are heaving at a dwarf plum tree with good-sized branches. The fruit is raining down to the ground, where the children's feet grind them into a fine mush.

1. Based on the first law of correction, on which category of wrong behavior did the children's behavior fall? Please explain your answer.

2. Based on the second law of correction, what type of education will prevent this behavior in the future?

3. Does the third law of correction apply to this situation? Please explain your answer.

4. Based on the fourth law of correction, what action is necessary to help bring closure to the children's wrong? Explain.

5. Based on the fifth law of correction, what can be done about the damaged plums?

Scenario Two

You catch six-year-old Nicole sneaking through the house playing hide-and-seek. You've already told all the children, including Nicole, not to play in the house. But her big brother, Nate, had just done the same thing only minutes before. His behavior had resulted in a broken lamp. Nicole hasn't broken anything.

1. Based on the first law of correction, into which category of wrong behavior did Nicole's behavior fall? What about Nate's behavior? Please explain your answer.

2. Based on the second law of correction, what could you do to help educate both children? Please explain your answer based on the second law.

3. Based on the third law of correction, what should the parents consider?

4. Based on the fourth law of correction, what action is necessary to help bring closure to Nicole's action? Please explain your answer.

5. Based on the fifth law of correction, what should be done about the broken lamp?

WHAT DID HAPPEN

Because these were actual events, we thought it would be useful to record what the authority figures actually did in these scenarios.

Scenario One

In the plum tree incident, we were dealing with childishness. Kara and R.J., the four-year-olds in question, had no malicious intent to do harm, nor an understanding of the cause and effect of their actions. They did not equate their present action as having significant meaning to others. However, though Kara and R.J.'s actions were void of malice, they nevertheless did bring injury to another's property.

Grandma took both children with their sticks and showed them what they did wrong. She then took them to another tree, the grapefruit tree, and showed them how wrong it would be to strike this fruit. She extended the lesson to the rose bushes. "You don't strike the plums, the grapefruit, or the roses," she said.

Additionally, the children lost the privilege of playing with their magical sticks and had to pick up all the plums. Finally, the children were directed to grandpa where they both apologized "for knocking down your plums, Grandpa." Since that time, neither we nor their parents have ever faced that behavior again.

Scenario Two

Although it was a costly accident, Nate's behavior was just that: an accident. His actions were considered childish, not defiant. Nonetheless, he was required to help clean up the mess. He was also at an age which made it appropriate for him to help pay something toward a new lamp. This was part of the learning experience. Although he did not mean harm, Nate had to learn to accept responsibility for his unintentional actions as well as the intentional ones.

Nicole's behavior, on the other hand, was not childish, but defiant. She simply ignored the instructions previously given. For her complete disregard of the instructions, she was punished. The logical consequence applied taught her the importance of submitting to parental leadership. She lost the privilege of playing the game.

Nate was guided to apologize to his parents, sharing how sorry he was for his carelessness. Nicole was guided to seek forgiveness for her rebellious heart actions. Both children were returned to the right path.

Chapter Nine

The Best Form of Correction— Prevention

*a*ll too often, parents rush the process of growing up. Too soon, mom or even grandma is signing up Samantha for tap class, simply because she twirled around the kitchen. But when she gets to the Tender Tappers lesson, Samantha runs to the bathroom five times, gets a drink after each spin, and generally disrupts the handful of hopeful Ginger Rogerses.

Samantha is just being a child. She has no concept of the money and time others have invested in this endeavor. And she is clearly out of her league. Mom is left coercing, correcting, and dealing with tears before each hour ends. This didn't need to happen.

There are many excellent methods of correction available to *Childwise* parents, but ultimately the best form of parental correction is prevention. There is no better way to deal with behavior problems than by preventing them in the first place. Parents may find themselves correcting misbehavior that could have easily been avoided had they first considered the principles of prevention.

It is even possible that parents, by overlooking prevention, may actually be encouraging misbehavior in their children. If a parent puts a child in a situation in which he is likely to have a problem being obedient, who is really to blame for the disobedience?

That's not to say that parents should shield their children from all potentially difficult situations. That would be the equivalent of child-proofing the home instead of home-proofing the child. But parents should take the idea of prevention into consideration when considering activities for their children. Just as you wouldn't send a recovering alcoholic into a bar to test his resolve, so it may not be wise to send your excitable child into a McDonald's play area where the other kids are running around with out-of-control ecstasy.

GROWTH AND LEARNING

Throughout your child's life, two processes continue to dominate: growth and learning. Growth refers to the biological processes of life. Learning refers to the mental processes, which includes moral development. In both processes, the building blocks are progressive. Each stage of development depends on the successful completion of the previous stage. You cannot rush the fruit.

CHILDWISE PRINCIPLE #11

Allowing a child to progress into his new and expanding world in an orderly fashion greatly enhances learning and decreases the need for correction.

In a child's developing world, it is the gradual assimilation of many perceptions that gives rise to the formation of ideas. Since learning comes in progressive stages, training should be equally progressive. The duty of parents is to channel the child into a learning environment that translates information into understanding. That environment cannot be so big that the child gets lost in it nor too restrictive that all creative thought is stifled. There is a place of balance to be sought. There, learning is maximized and the need for correction is minimized. The aim of this chapter is to help you find that balance for your family.

COVERING THE BASICS

Creation is orderly. The planets travel predictable courses, ocean tides move in and out in patterns charted to the minute, the four seasons are all part of the earth's sleep/wake cycle. In all living things, there are orderly and predictable stages of growth in the maturation process.

Given the witness of creation, the inclination of nature, and the consistent growth patterns in children, it stands to reason that order would be valuable in the life of a child, too. This is particularly true in the areas of sleep and healthy eating patterns. Both are prerequisites for optimal development. Both are part of good behavior management. They are in the category of prevention.

Take sleep, for example. Did your child actually wake up today rested enough to begin a new day of development? Parents often think only in terms of sleep time and wake time: She's asleep or she's awake. Yet there actually exists a gradation of sleep and wake time. Sleep ranges from deep sleep to active sleep to groggy wake time to complete wakefulness. She starts the day best when she emerges from the complete sequence. Optimum learning occurs when the child is at optimum wakefulness, which only happens when she has experienced optimum sleep.

More and more studies are confirming what our grandmothers knew intuitively just a generation ago. Preschool and school-aged children who suffer from a deficiency of healthy sleep have a pervasive fatigue that affects alertness. Such a child becomes inattentive, unable to concentrate, easily distracted, and physically hyperactive.

Researchers have found a clear relationship between poor sleep habits and misbehavior. One significant report found that children who sleep less than ten hours in a twenty-four hour period may be more likely to throw temper tantrums than those who get more sleep. The study also indicated that children who got less sleep also had a 25 percent greater chance of developing a psychiatric disorder such as oppositional defiant disorder (ODD) and attention deficit disorder (ADD).[11]

In contrast, children whose parents help them develop healthy sleep habits are optimally awake and optimally alert to interact with their environment. They are more self-assured, happier, and demonstrate longer attention spans. As a result, they are better learners.

Good rest is a great place to begin your parenting. Tonight's rest may be your best ally in preventing bad behavior tomorrow. Get them to bed! Enforce naps and reasonable bedtimes. Your preschooler certainly does not possess the wisdom to govern this area of his life.

If you can't get your three-year-old to lie in bed for his midday rest, most likely he controls far more in your home than shut-eye. Take back the reins and manage his little life for the sake of his development. Otherwise you will end up frustrated and frazzled later over issues which erupt from his exhaustion. Sometimes what looks to be senseless defiance is really just a child's cry for someone to take control and tuck him into bed. Do this for both of you.

A second wonderful place to parent is in the area of food. Consider the nourishment you put into your growing bundle of energy. The body is the perfect machine, able to cope and make the most of its environment. Yet so many people stress the system with valueless fuel.

When the little guy starts fussing, there's nothing like a buck's worth of junk from the snack bar to settle him down, right? But only while he's chewing. When the sugar-laden treat is gone, the fussing boy is more like a firecracker. One small spark can set him off. What happened? If the boy is edgy and agitated, he may truly be hungry. But his body is calling out not for junk, but for something of value to give his system the fuel to function properly. Bad behavior and an ornery attitude can sometimes be traced back to poor nutrition.

A healthy diet and plentiful sleep are two of your strongest helps in preventing bad behavior before it has a chance to form. Make certain your child's diet is suited to her makeup, providing pure nutrients for her to grow. And manage her sleep so that optimal wakefulness is achieved. Both will facilitate learning and good behavior.

Doing this may seem like a burden to you. After all, what could be easier than swinging by Burger King on the way home? "Oh, no," you say. "These writers are telling me I've got to cook real food, serve healthy snacks, and enforce meal times and sleep times? Forget it. They don't know my schedule."

You're right, we don't. And of course you'll need to adapt what we say here to your situation. But we believe that steps you take toward this ideal will help you in the long run by minimizing the behavior problems you *will* spend energy on—problems that might've been avoided if the child had been eating and sleeping right.

PARENTING IN AND OUTSIDE THE FUNNEL

There is a consensus in the world of childhood experts that when a child is at peace with his environment his learning potential increases, learning disorders abate, and dysfunctional behaviors diminish. So what happens when a child is consistently placed in an environment that is *not* age-appropriate? What does it do to a child if she is always smaller than the chairs, the toilets, and the other kids? What does it do if she's always larger? What happens to a child who is given too many freedoms too early? What about a child who is free to direct his own life without parental account-ability?

Please take note of the funnel diagram on the next page. The narrow stem represents the early stages of parenting, when the child is very young. The wider part represents the expanding growth, maturity, and gradual freedoms the child is able to handle.

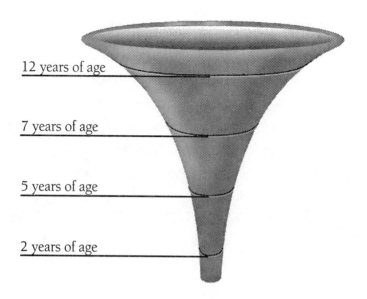

12 years of age

7 years of age

5 years of age

2 years of age

A common mistake is to parent outside the funnel in the early years. In an effort to give the child confidence, parents sometimes allow their children behaviors or freedoms that are neither age-appropriate nor in harmony with the child's moral and intellectual capabilities.

To allow a two-year-old the freedoms appropriate to a five-year-old—or to allow a five-year-old the freedoms appropriate to a twelve-year-old—is to parent outside the funnel. It forces a child to carry an oversized burden he is not prepared to carry. Contrary to child-centered thinking, such freedoms do not facilitate healthy learning patterns. Instead, they create oversized problems for an undersized child. And please note, the problem does not start with the child, but with the parents who have thrust him into a situation bigger than he can handle at his age.

BIG BRITCHES AND WISE EYES

No concerned parent would give a three-year-old a sharp knife and let him peal his own apple. But most parents would consider granting that freedom to a ten-year-old. The difference, obviously, is in regard to the age and sense of responsibility in the children.

As parents, we are very protective of our children when it comes to health and safety issues. We would never let our four-year-old climb the ladder leaning against the second-story window. Nor would we intentionally put our children in dangerous environments. We would not let our five-year-old spray weed poison around the house just because it looks like fun. If we granted such freedoms on a regular basis, our children would probably assume a false sense of confidence in their own abilities and judgments. It is that unjustified confidence that can lead to reckless behavior and tragedy.

When was the last time you heard these clichés: "That kid is too big for his britches" or "That child is just wise in her own eyes—and it's going to get her in trouble one of these days"? Beneath these less-than-complimentary statements lies a legitimate concern.

As it relates to children and child training, the warning speaks against creating the false impression in the mind of a child that she is able to do all, say all, and go to all places without parental guidance or approval. Simply put, this is a child who has been granted too many freedoms of self-governance too early.

It is our firm conviction, based on the thousands of parents we work with, that more conflicts arise out of this "wise in your own eyes" attitude than any other single factor in parenting. A child that acts wise in his own eyes is a child living above his age-appropriate level of freedoms. He is outside the funnel.

Practically speaking, what are some of the ways children become wise in their own eyes? Here are the three most common ways:

1. Parents grant too many decision-making freedoms.

2. Parents grant too many physical freedoms.

3. Parents grant too many verbal freedoms.

DECISION-MAKING FREEDOMS—TOO MANY CHOICES TOO EARLY

Choices. It is the cry of our day. "Give children plenty of choices in the early years," says the theorist. "Let the child decide and he will learn to make wise ones when he grows up." That outcome may not be exactly sustained by the evidence. Our prisons are full of people who made choices all their lives. Contrary to the theorist's opinion, having choices and the freedom to be self-determining does not mean people will make the right choices.

There is no question that children can be guided into good patterns of decision-making by learning how to make wise choices as children. Allowing a child to make his own decisions is both educational and rewarding. But good decision-making skills do not rely on the natural inclination of the child, but upon careful parental guidance. It is crucial for parents to take leadership in this matter. Without guidance, the child will grow up making decisions based only on his natural inclinations: pursuing pleasure and avoiding pain.

Here, too, parenting philosophies help or hinder the development of wise decision-making. Neither over-controlling nor under-controlling methods are helpful approaches for teaching choices. The first tends to deny the child sufficient opportunities for making choices at all. This suppresses within her an age-appropriate sense of control and the educational opportunities to learn through wise and unwise decisions. The second philosophy overindulges the child with too many choices, too early.

As it relates to decision-making freedoms, the majority of parents today are not guilty of overly suppressing a child's choices. On the contrary, most homes run in the opposite direction. At a typical three-year-old's birthday party, guests are offered four beverage selections before they even sit down. And then they have to choose between napkin colors, fork colors, plate styles, size of cake piece, corner or middle piece, and chair or floor.

Why do mothers do this?

Then there's shoes. Moms are paralyzed in picking out new sneakers for their children. They have to secure the approval of their preschoolers, who are more apt to squeeze their tootsies into the latest trend than something half the price.

And what about the breakfast, lunch, or dinner choices you put before your children? Go ahead and count the number of different cereal boxes in your kitchen cabinet. Possibly a variety sits on your shelf because you know exactly what would happen the moment you put out the cornflakes and said, "This is for breakfast; Mom has decided."

We would expect to find this phenomenon in child-centered homes. But we have been surprised to find it in even the best parent-directed homes. For whatever reason, the tendency to overwhelm our children with choices seems to have very strong appeal.

Here's why we believe it's wrong: Offering unlimited choices is one way children become wise in their own eyes. You cannot give a child unlimited decision-making powers without also giving him an unwielding sense of power.

Some would argue, "Ah, but isn't that what we're supposed to do—empower our children?" *Empower* is such a loaded term. Yes, you want your child to feel confident about his abilities to make choices for himself. Transferring the ability to make right choices from parent to child is what we're all about. But don't forget the age-appropriateness factor or the fact that parents are to be leading your family. The child should not be empowered to make everyone get out of one car and into another because he wants to ride in the blue one.

It is our experience that a child with too many choices grows up to be insecure, frightened, and difficult to manage. He becomes hostile when demands are placed on him that he does not agree with. Even reasonable demands become a source of potential conflict. It doesn't matter if it is "Drink your juice" or "First finish your homework"; conflict for these children is inevitable. They simply cannot handle *not* having a choice.

Please keep this in perspective. We are not saying you should hold back all choices from your children. We are suggesting that you beware of prematurely granting freedoms to decide on issues that the child is not developmentally or intellectually or emotionally able to handle. If a child is ready to make choices about major life issues, then they really don't need mom and dad around.

FREEDOMS FROM A CHILD'S PERSPECTIVE

Remember, the real problem is not giving children choices, but doing so prematurely and to the point of overindulgence. Consider what we are about to say from a child's perspective and developing worldview. The following scenario demonstrates our point.

It's breakfast time. You're in the kitchen when four-year-old Jason enters. You've just poured orange juice in the red cup, but, when Jason notices, he politely reminds you that his cup is the blue one with the starship. You smile and make the switch. He also informs you of his desire to have grape juice this morning instead of orange juice. No problem. Both are healthy. You pour the orange juice in your glass and grape juice in his. As you begin to butter Jason's toast, he decides that today he would like jam instead of butter. Well, the buttered toast can be for you. You put another slice of bread into the toaster for Jason. Putting jam on it is no big deal.

After breakfast, it's reading time. You say to Jason, "Sit here on my right and I will read you a story." But Jason decides to sit on your left near the big pillow. Then you pick up a book and open it on your lap. But Jason picks another story, his favorite, and off the two of you go for a fifteen-minute adventure. After reading time, your son informs you, "Mom, I'm going to play on my swing set." And off he goes.

"Okay," you say to his back. "Thanks for letting me know."

So far the morning has been rather easy—no conflicts or trials. Who said parenting was hard? At noon, you instruct Jason to put away his toys and get ready for lunch. "Mommy," Jason says, "I decided to have lunch later. I'm playing with my trucks now." You repeat your instructions firmly. Jason is equally firm. Things begin to escalate. Soon your little tempest becomes a storm, and a small skirmish becomes an outright battle of wills.

Frustrated and discouraged, you ask yourself the question: Why am I experiencing such behavior from my son? After all, have I not been fair with him all morning, meeting his needs and desires? Why am I getting such resistance and defiance to my instructions? This choice thing is not working as the experts said.

Let's look back over the morning from Jason's perspective. Who decided that it would be the blue cup and not the red cup? The child. Who decided it would be grape juice and not orange juice? The child. Who decided that it would be jam instead of butter? Again, the child. Who decided where he would sit and what he would read? The child. Who decided what happened after reading time? The child.

Jason has been making every decision for himself. He has gotten his way all day long. He is lord of all he surveys and master of his own destiny. Every time mom wants X, Jason chooses Y, and mom changes to Y. Jason may even change to Z. So why on earth should he think mom had any voice in the matter whatsoever? Mom's desires for him are merely suggestions, points of departure.

For Jason, having the final word is a way of life. Mom's instructions are an intrusion. At the ripe old age of four, Jason has become wise in his own eyes. But look at the bright side; he really feels empowered. It is this false feeling of self-reliance that gets children in trouble. They tend to go places physically and verbally where they should not go.

Giving too many choices too early will push the child outside the funnel in a jiffy. Conflict like we saw between Jason and his mom is born out of the fact that young children cannot handle the *power* associated with decision-making prior to the establishment of a self-regulating, moral conscience. Indeed, in their heart of hearts, they don't even want it. They don't want to be the parent, they just want to be kids.

Jason has no way of differentiating between nonmoral choices (red cup/blue cup) and moral ones requiring obedience. From his perspective, saying no to mom's instructions at mealtime is no different than saying no to mom's selection of juice. The privilege of saying no to the orange juice is transferred to the right of saying no to any of mom's instructions. Even in children, power corrupts.

Addicted to Choice

Can your child handle not being given a choice for what is served at breakfast? We're not asking whether she will live or not, because of course she will, but whether or not she will "go ballistic" if she doesn't get to choose between Fruit Loops and Sugar Pops.

You can know if your child is addicted to choice by simply observing what happens when all choices are taken away. For example, if at breakfast you offered milk in a clear glass, cereal (your choice) in a plain bowl, and a piece of buttered toast on a plate, would your child accept this without complaint?

Try it tomorrow morning. If she comes to the table and accepts your meal decision, then your child is probably able to handle a degree of freedom in decision-making in this area. If, on the other hand, she protests your breakfast selection, grumbles, complains, cries, and refuses to eat, you may have a problem. There is a strong possibility that you have a child who is addicted to choice.

A child who is addicted to choice cannot emotionally cope in life when no choice is available to him. Therein lies the sad legacy of poorly thought-out parenting philosophies: Thinking they're helping their child succeed, parents can be setting him up to suffer.

Does your child fall apart when you deny him an impulsive desire? Does he debate you all the time? Does he always have a better idea? When you give specific instructions, does your child struggle to submit? Consider the possibility that he is addicted to deciding for himself—he is addicted to choice. You may have given him too many freedoms too early.

This is no way to prepare him for life. The real world will not bow to his every whim nor will it always give choices. You are not doing anyone—yourself, the child, or society—any favors by raising up a child who is addicted to choice.

That's Me! What Can I Do?

If you find yourself in this section, don't despair! You can treat this addiction. First, evaluate just how bad the addiction is. From mealtime to reading time to bedtime, are you continually offering choices? Is it a way of life for you and your child?

Second, get the whole family to work together on limiting

choices. If mom and dad are scaling way back on choices but gramma and grampa aren't, there will be an unevenness to the child's training (and he will likely want to spend more and more time at gramma's).

You must narrow the boundaries. One way to do this is to take back ownership of those freedoms you have given out prematurely. Instead of letting your four-year-old decide what he will have for breakfast, *you* decide.

Sit your little one down and explain what you're up to. "Mary, Mommy has been letting you make all your decisions. From now on, Mom will start helping you make them. Some days, I will ask you what you want for breakfast. Other days Mommy will just pick for you. The same goes for what you're going to wear, what you're going to watch, and how you're going to play."

The breakfast conversation might sound something like this:

"Mary, today you are having cereal for breakfast."

"But Mom, I want pancakes!"

"No, breakfast today is Mom's decision. Mary, I need to hear a 'Yes, Mommy' from you."

"Yes, Mommy."

There will be days when the child can choose, especially as she demonstrates contentment with you being in charge. But right now you must take back ownership of this vitally important lost ground. You can give her back the freedom to choose after she has learned to accept your choices without insurrection—or even grumbling or whining. Most days, mom and/or dad will decide what's for dinner, what is to be worn, when there will be organized play time, and when it is time to come inside. You want your children to find wisdom in your authority and not in their own eyes.

But what happens when your child throws a fit because he did not get his sugar-laden Choco-Bombs? How do you handle correction in that moment when you are just starting to reclaim this territory?

Answer: nothing. Nothing at all. Consider this moment a chance to take inventory of just how deeply seated the addiction is. Your natural temptation will be to try to fix the problem right in that moment. But if you do, expect that both you and your child will have a miserable day. You must do more than fix the moment. You must change the child's perspective—and maybe your own—on your right to rule, decide about, and guide her little life.

Where should you start to make this transition? First, finish reading *Childwise*. Then go back to chapter 2. Get with your spouse on the couch everyday for your fifteen-minute couch time. Begin creating a new impression for your child of what mom and dad are about. "Hey, they aren't just my overindulgent caregivers, they are a team committed to loving each other and me—not just me, me, me."

Then go back to chapter 7 and see how you're doing with your verbal instructions and your child's response. Start working on the "Yes, mom" and "Yes, dad" comeback. Do not underestimate the power of this little response in retraining your child's heart. It actually creates a willingness in your child to follow your lead.

Finally, be consistent. Reclaiming leadership in your home—breaking the addiction to choosing—can take anywhere from three days to three weeks or more. Changing ingrained patterns of behavior takes time. But children are resilient. In their hearts, they want to be led.

Once Upon a Time in Real Life

This is from a letter we've recently received.

> Gary,
>
> I wanted to tell you how the "addicted to choice" material has impacted our three-year-old daughter. This information came to us at a most opportune time. Our daughter was beginning to have uncharacteristic temper tantrums. She had two fits in which she was throwing things, hitting, kicking, screaming. Way out of character for our little girl.
>
> When I found your material on choices, I started paying attention at home. I noticed that both my wife and I offered her choices on almost everything. My wife would regularly fix our daughter special meals if she thought she wouldn't like what we were having. Our little girl got to choose what she was going to wear, what she was going to play, etc.
>
> I told my wife about your choice addiction idea, and she wanted to try your advice. When she told me about the second tantrum, I decided it was time for a change. We explained to our daughter what we were going to do and

then radically restricted her choices.

Something amazing has happened: our daughter is *much* happier. She's sleeping better, eating better, and behaving better. It's almost as if she is *glad* to have the limits. I expected her behavior to improve and the tantrums to stop, but I didn't expect her to enjoy the restrictions. She even reminds us if we give her a choice she feels she shouldn't have!

VERBAL AND PHYSICAL FREEDOMS

Do you let your three-year-old go into the backyard to play without asking permission? Do you let your five-year-old decide for herself when she can go next door to play with her friend? Think through your day. How many times do you hear your child say, "Mom, I'm going to…" rather than, "Mom, may I…?" Is your child *asking* you to do things or just *telling* you what he's going to do?

How we speak to our children and how we allow them to speak to us greatly affect patterns of behavior. Again, remember that this chapter is devoted to prevention. We want to prevent poor behavior by what we do and say. What we say and what we allow our child to say to us represent verbal definitions of the boundaries of the child's perception of self, self-reliance, and self-governance.

The child who customarily *tells* you what she is going to do is assuming a level of decision-making freedom which she may or may not have. And if this continues, it is because her parents have allowed her to take this ground and hold it. Parents must evaluate whether the freedom to decide in the matter in question is age-appropriate.

If your five-year-old believes she has the freedom to come and go at will, then what will stop her from wandering off when you're at the playground, at the mall, or at the beach? It is not just the wandering off that is our concern, but the child's confirmed sense of independence from parental guidance at such a tender age. This is another type of freedom that can push the child outside the funnel.

There is nothing wrong with a child wanting to go next door to play. Nor is there anything inherently wrong with a parent choosing to grant such a desire. The problem is over the question of who is ultimately deciding.

There is a simple technique you can use to keep this problem at bay. Have your child ask permission rather than informing you of his decision. "Mom, may I go...?" rather than, "Mom, I'm going..." Young children need more from their parents than simply guidance. They also need the security that parental leadership brings into their world. Seeking permission helps a child realize his dependence on your leadership. It also helps prevent a child from becoming wise in his own eyes.

One warning: this technique will only work if you actually play your parental role. If your child asks permission to go next door and you say no, you may witness a case of spontaneous combustion right there in your living room. If the child throws a tantrum (or threatens to in front of your company) and you give in, you haven't made an adjustment at all. The child is still *telling* you what he's going to do—you've just changed the vocabulary.

If a child never has to ask for permission, he will (rightly) assume that it means he has the freedom to do whatever he wants, whenever he wants to, regardless of ownership or ability. How many of these children we see in society today! Shopping malls, amusement parks, and airports are full of them. A child who never has to ask permission is without restraint. And that's something you would never want to wish on any child, least of all yours.

Verbal freedoms are more than just a child claiming her right to come and go at will. It is also a problem of tone. Listen to the way your child talks to you and to others. Is she characterized by being bossy? How does her tone sound? Is she sassy to her siblings? Does she always need to have the last word? Is her speech demanding? "Mommy, now! I want it right now!" Does she routinely tell you, "No," leaving you to wonder who's really in charge? These are all classic signs of a child with too many verbal freedoms.

If your child lives under the impression that he is a verbal peer with you, your instructions and desire for compliance move from a need-to-do list to a wish list. Mom and dad, let us remind you: You are the parents. Control the tone that flows from your precious child's little lips.

Fixing this problem requires pulling in the verbal boundaries. Don't worry, you will not be stifling your child's freedom of expression—just modifying the character behind it. Here again is that workable but simple solution: many parents have found great success in this area by insisting on a, "Yes, Mommy."

If you are in the retraining process and you know your child is going to verbally battle your every request, then establish in your instructions the parameters of his response. "Timmy, Mommy wants you to pick up your toys now. And Timmy, Mommy wants to hear only a 'Yes, Mommy' coming from your lips."

"But, but, but—"

"No, Timmy. 'Yes, Mommy' is the only response you are allowed to give me right now."

"Yes, Mommy."

Other mothers have approached this challenge this way. If Timmy answers with "But, but, but…" mom can say, "Timmy, you do not have the freedom to talk back to your mother."

Add some resolve to your request and the problem is usually fixed fairly quickly. The new habit of speech begins to override the old.

SUMMARY

Prevention is the best form of correction. You should continually evaluate what you allow your child to do and whether those freedoms are appropriate considering his age, understanding, and abilities. Are you giving him inappropriate freedoms?

Let freedoms be handed out carefully as the child demonstrates contentment with your authority and responsibility in previous freedoms given. Granting freedoms consistent with a child's level of self-control equals developmental harmony.

Harmony! What a beautiful word for a child. The word *harmony* means putting the parts into a pleasing and orderly whole.

That is exactly what parents should strive to do with their children. That comes when you move your child from age-appropriate restraint to age-appropriate freedoms.

Freedoms come gradually: from the playpen, to the backyard, to the neighborhood, to the world at large. As your child demonstrates responsible behavior and sound judgment, he earns another level of freedom. This type of training results in a child who is a joy to everyone and who has achieved a sense of affirmation within himself.

QUESTIONS FOR REVIEW

1. Briefly explain how allowing a child to progress into his new and expanding world in an orderly fashion enhances learning.

2. What is implied by the phrase, "parenting outside the funnel"?

3. How does the way we speak to our children or allow them to speak to us influence patterns of behavior?

4. What technique can you use to change telling to asking? What is the catch?

5. What does it mean for a child to be wise in his own eyes?

6. Explain what "addicted to choice" means.

Chapter Ten

Transferring Ownership of Behavior to Children

*I*t's called follow-through, completion, "sticktoitiveness," perseverance, finishing the task at hand, and taking full ownership. Ultimately, this is what we want our children to be characterized by. When a task is placed in front of them, they know how to complete it without prompting, bribing, threatening, or a continual barrage of reminders. Unfortunately, sometimes parents are their own worst enemy when it comes to molding these virtues into their children.

It's the same thing every day. Driving home from kindergarten, you gently remind your little one that when you get home, he is to unpack his snack bag on his trek through the kitchen. Oh, and he is to lay all papers on the counter before taking the backpack upstairs. Did he bring home any papers for mom to sign?

Then, as the garage door lifts, the dog comes thundering out and your thoughts get distracted. The water bowl needs refilling. And wait, today is trash day. Meanwhile, your little guy takes off for the swing set.

Hours later you discover the backpack lying in the dirt in the backyard, stuffed to the gills with papers, wet painted portraits, and one smelly, brown banana peel. "Oh," moans mom. "How many times must I remind you? Your backpack first."

The backpack isn't really the problem—it's what it represents. It's a symbol of the child's lack of follow-through. It's sitting there in the dirt, filled with stuff, because mom wasn't there to prod Junior to complete the task at hand—to remind him to follow through completely.

Mom yearns to turn this situation around, but how? Until mom and dad learn how to transfer ownership responsibility for follow-through behavior to Junior, Junior has no reason to accept responsibility or accountability for his actions. No child will ever reach self-generated initiative as long as mom and dad are always prompting.

The goal of this chapter is to teach you how to pass to your child a sense of behavioral ownership and how to implant a self-generated sense of responsibility. You want your child to be characterized by diligence in following through with his own actions, mistakes, messes, and misdeeds.

But how do you get there? You will know that you have arrived when you are no longer the catalyst for your children's initiative. Constantly reminding a child what is right, wrong, or expected not only frustrates parents but robs the child of any motivation to follow through for himself. From the child's perspective, why take ownership of today's lesson if I'm going to be schooled in it again tomorrow?

Instilling a "sticktoitive" virtue into your children is not as difficult as it might appear on paper. There are two governing principles that cannot be ignored in the process.

Principle One: Parents Own All Behaviors Until the Child Is Both Intellectually Ready and Physically Capable to Take Ownership

We touched on this point in earlier chapters. This principle acknowledges that parents are responsible for their young children's messes, mistakes, and misdeeds. If your two-year-old drops pancake syrup on the family pet, you do not assign him the task of giving the dog a bath. If your four-year-old accidentally spills the open can of paint on the garage floor, you don't sit back and let her clean up the mess. She will only make a bigger mess.

So what happens? You step in. In these cases, the child's mess is your mess. His mistakes and accidents belong to you. You're responsible because the child is not old enough to be responsible for rectifying the problems his actions created.

Principle Two: In Child Training, Behavioral Outcomes Belong to Parents Until Ownership Can Be Transferred to the Child

The question parents must wrestle with is which behaviors fall under their management and what behaviors should be managed by the child. In the examples above, mom and dad own the outcomes because of the age of the children involved. But as children grow, their capacity to assume responsibility and take ownership also grows. While a two-year-old could not give the dog a bath, an eight-year-old could. A twelve-year-old might be able to clean spilled paint a four-year-old couldn't.

So how do you know when to make behavioral ownership transfers? To answer that question, we need to consider the two phases of training: *preaccountability* and *accountability*.

PREACCOUNTABILITY AND ACCOUNTABILITY TRAINING

The preaccountability phase is the period of training in which the child is in the process of learning specific skills, courtesies, and patterns of right behavior. During this phase, the child is not held fully responsible for his own actions.

For example, there was a time when mom used to put out the paint set and coloring book for three-year-old Lucy. Afterwards, mom cleaned up the mess because Lucy wasn't ready for that task. This is in the preaccountability phase. But the day came when mom began to show Lucy how she could get her paint set down from the shelf, lay out the newspaper on the kitchen table, and then, after paint time, clean up after herself. This is making the transition to the accountability phase.

Mom is teaching responsible behavior for a specific task. As Lucy grows and becomes more responsible, she is taught to take more and more ownership of her own behavior. Eventually, Lucy— not mom—is held accountable for her own paint-time activities. Mom has properly transferred it to Lucy.

Your child will learn new behaviors and courtesies throughout childhood. Therefore this process—preaccountability training, followed by accountability training—will be repeated throughout your child's development. It starts with the introduction of a behavioral expectation, allows time for assimilation of the new behavior, and then transitions to the child accepting ownership of the behavior. The preaccountability phase might last months for some tasks and some children, minutes for others.

In a previous chapter, we introduced the concept of teaching your child to respond to an instruction by saying, "Yes, mom" or "Yes, dad." If a parent starts this training with an eighteen-month-old, the child cannot be expected to take ownership of this behavior for a considerable time. Possibly a year or more will pass before the child consistently gives this response. If, on the other hand, you introduce this concept to a four-year-old, he should be consistently complying within a few weeks.

MONKEYS ON YOUR BACK

Remember Blake's mom? She threatened the child repeatedly that she was going to get on the airplane without him, and he finally said, "Have a nice trip." This mother had taught her child that she could safely be ignored. Her habit of repeating her instructions, redrawing lines in the sand, and spewing out empty threats was obvious to anyone standing by.

There is another, more subtle, form of this ineffective parenting style. What happens when the reminders aren't repeated in successive sentences but over a period of hours, days, or weeks? If every day, you have to remind your child to put his schoolbag away, you are acting just like Blake's mom. The difference is only in the form of your threatening and repeating, not in substance.

No wonder the child doesn't appropriate your instructions: there are no consequences for neglecting them, and anyway they'll be repeated tomorrow so why remember today? At what point will you stop reminding?

CHILDWISE PRINCIPLE #12

*Constantly reminding a child to do what is
expected only means you have no expectation.*

When parents continue to instruct and remind their children how to behave after accountability training has been achieved, they are taking back ownership of a behavior that should no longer belong to them. When parents do this, they pick up unwelcome behavioral "monkeys."

Monkeys are a great analogy for what is happening here. Monkeys can be cute little critters or bothersome pests, especially when they start climbing all over you, making you weary from their weight and busyness. We use the monkey analogy because monkeys love jumping. In parenting there are behavioral monkeys that love jumping from child to parent. That's the wrong direction. Your goal is to get rid of the monkeys not collect them.

In the early years, parents carry all the monkeys. But there comes a day when your child is ready to take ownership of his own actions, behaviors, and attitudes. Remember Junior's backpack sitting in the dirt? Responsibility for the backpack was Junior's. But it wasn't always so. There was a period of preaccountability when he was learning to become responsible with his papers and backpack.

Mom and dad owned that behavior then. But once Junior learned and understood what was required of him and he was capable of following through, the ownership monkey was passed to him.

There are certain behavioral expectations that you passed to your children a long time ago. Knowing how to clean their room, pick up after themselves, extend a courtesy, or being responsible to remember to feed the cat. Once the ownership papers have been transferred, the monkey belongs to the child. The problem is, all of these monkeys love to jump back to their original carriers—mom and dad.

When do behavioral monkeys jump from the child back to the parent? When a parent continues to assume ownership of a behavior that rightly belongs to the child and that happens whenever you continually remind a child of a responsibility that he is to be managing. You know you have too many monkeys when you become increasingly frustrated and annoyed at the child's lack of initiative in assuming responsibility for his behavior. Multiply the number of monkeys by the number of children you have. Then realize the older your children, the bigger the monkeys. We know parents of teens who daily carry around dozens of gorillas. Let's put some flesh on our analogy.

Darece's Story

"I'm tired of always reminding them!" Have your ever whispered that phrase—or shouted it? When Darece first heard the monkey concept, breakfast time immediately came to mind. "My five children all have little chores to do before they sit down for breakfast, but I found myself asking every morning, 'Did you make your bed?' 'Put your books in your schoolbag.' 'Nicholas, did you feed the dog?' With five kids, there is bound to be a 'No, not yet, Mom' in there somewhere."

Darece resolved the problem in a big way. She sat the kids down and announced that she no longer was going to remind them each morning of what was expected. Instead, they simply did not have the freedom to sit down for breakfast if they did not first take care of their morning responsibilities. In fact, a great phrase to fend off monkeys begins just that way: "Do you have the freedom to…?"

The next morning, ten-year-old Nicholas came out of his room headed for the breakfast table. He looked at mom, then the breakfast table, and then stopped in his tracks. With a smile he said: "Ah, I don't think I have the freedom to be here right now. I'll be right back, Mom." Off Nicholas went to take care of a forgotten chore.

What a relief for Darece. For months she'd repeated herself every morning. By always asking her children if their chores were done, beds were made, school lunches were ready, and papers were signed, she was collecting all their monkeys. In so doing, she had taken back ownership responsibilities that belonged to the kids. By 8:00 A.M., with five children in the house, mom had picked up a dozen monkeys. And the day had just begun.

As long as mom was there to remind them what to do, they never had to be concerned about doing on their own. In the child's view of things, it is easy to see what is going on. If Nicholas gets to the table and mom is too busy to ask about his chores, he wins. The worse thing that could happen is hearing mom's reminder and having to go back and do what was expected. All this was solved by the simple little phrase: "Do you have the freedom to…?"

MONKEY REPELLENT

It is helpful to think of privileges in terms of freedoms which children can earn or lose. For example, your six-year-old has been playing in his room for the morning and decides he now wants to play outside. He heads for the slides, but mom intercepts him. "Where are you going, Danny?"

"Outside to play."

The next questions that seems to flow from the lips of most moms go like this: "You were just in your room. Did you pick up your toys? How about your puzzle, is that put away? And all of your little army men, are they put back in the box?"

With her checklist of questions, the ownership for a clean room just jumped back on mom's shoulders. If Danny's mom is going to keep reminding him of what should have been done, then he never has to take the initiative to do it in the first place. Like Nicholas above, what could he lose? If he gets caught, the worst that will happen is that he will have to sit under mom's lecture about responsibility and be forced to march back to his room. Danny knows there is a good chance that mom won't ask at all— all for the better, in Danny's thinking.

There is a better way to handle this. Instead of a checklist of questions, try some monkey repellent: "Danny, I know you where just playing in your room. Do you have the freedom to play outside right now?" With that question the burden (monkey) of responsibility for a clean room stays where it belongs—with Danny—because the thinking stays with Danny. Instead of mom telling him what needs to be done, Danny takes ownership of what needs to be done.

Eventually, Danny will learn that when he wants to leave one activity and go to another, mom is going to ask the big "Do you have the freedom" question. Just knowing that question is coming will serve as a wonderful catalyst to motivate any child to accept responsibility for the here and now. Instilling self-generated follow-through is a life skill worthy of any parent's attention.

Most children really do want to look you in the eye and honestly say, "Yes, Mom, I do have the freedom to play outside. My room is picked up, my homework is finished, and my chores are done."

If a child tells his parents that he has the freedom to do something and in reality he doesn't, consequences are necessary. In the above scenario, of course the child would need to pick up his toys. But that is not the consequence, since he was responsible to do that in the first place. After he picks up his toys, the consequence is imposed: He loses the freedom of going outside for a period of time to remind him to be honest the next time he is asked.

The phrase "Do you have the freedom to do that?" repels monkeys because it puts the burden back on the child. What burden? The burden of ownership. The child thinks, "What must I do before I have the freedom to do anything else?" Contrast the expectations associated with the "Do you have the freedom" question with the daily checklist of parental reminders. Which one do you think will provoke a child to greater initiative and follow-through?

With the first, you are teaching your child to be responsible. With the reminder, you are only correcting an obedience problem. Please note the difference between obedience training and responsibility training. Parents unintentionally tend to do more of the first and less of the second.

Obedience says: the child will do it when reminded. Responsibility says: the child will do it before he needs reminding. Which category of training would you rather be in? That is why we encourage you to seriously consider this ownership issue and the verbiage associated with it.

The simple question, "Danny, do you have the freedom?" forces him to *think*. *Well, do I?* He starts reviewing what mom or dad has just said. He looks around the room for things lying out or anything else that might trigger his memory. You'll be amazed at the things he comes up with that he needs to do first—things you weren't even aware of or had forgotten about. That's the sign of a bona fide conscience, and it's a beautiful thing to behold. An additional benefit is that children who develop this pattern of thinking become less susceptible to peer pressure because they are not dependent on others to do their thinking for them.

Starting Early

When working with a child who is still in the preaccountability phase of training, you can start introducing the concept of freedoms. Instead of asking, "Do you have the freedom to do that?" you would say, "Honey, you do not have the freedom to do that right now." It becomes a statement, not a question.

For example, your child wants to go outside and play, but you have just recently instructed him that when he is ready to leave one activity for another, he needs to put the first activity away. This is a new concept for him. Therefore, when he asks to go outside, mom would say, "You don't have the freedom to go outside until your toys are put away." Other examples would be, "You don't have the freedom to decide what you will wear today. That is a Mommy decision."

Remember principle one. Parents own all behaviors until the child is both ready and able to take ownership. Moms and dads own not only behaviors but decisions governing behaviors until they are able to successfully transfer the rights and responsibilities to the child. Someday, going outside to play, picking out school clothes, and visiting the refrigerator will be the child's decision. For the young ones, those behaviors still belong to mom and dad.

Now let's shift gears and consider the monkey principle with an older child.

Carly's Story

Carly found herself beyond irritation with her thirteen-year-old son, Michael. She felt she was continually reminding, even nagging, her son to do things he was supposed to do. One Saturday, a friend called and invited Michael over to play ball. With his hand over the receiver, Michael looked at his mom and asked, "Mom, may I go to Nate's house this afternoon?"

Normally, Carly would have asked him if he had completed his assigned chores, finished his homework due on Monday, and a litany of other dredged up commitments she was able to recall. This time, however, she instead said, "I don't know, Michael. Can you go?"

Michael looked at her, somewhat confused. "Well, I haven't finished my chores or swept the garage like Dad asked me to or started that paper that's due next week."

Carly was thinking to herself, *He knows exactly what he is supposed to be doing, so why do I keep on reminding him?*

Then, Michael said, "So, can I go?"

Somewhat amazed, Carly asked how he could even ask, knowing he hadn't done his work.

"Well," he said, "here's how it works. If I want to do something and you tell me no, I can start to argue with you, telling you how unfair you are and how you always want me to work and you never want me to have any fun, and keep arguing with you hoping that you might give in and let me go, which you usually do. And if you tell me yes, that works, too. I know I'll have to sit through a lecture when I get back—because while I'm gone you'll probably find out that I didn't do any of my chores—but it will be okay because I will have gotten to do what I wanted to do. Either way, I get to go."

You've got to hand it to this kid: he knows how to work the system.

"Well," Carly responded, "this time it's not going to work that way. I'm not going to decide this for you. You tell me whether or not you are free to go."

Michael was not happy about this. He followed his mom

around for some time trying to get her to tell him that he could go—or even that he couldn't. He desperately wanted the decision to be hers. She did not yield, however, and finally, he called his friend back and said he did not have the freedom to come over that day.

Let's look at what happened in this scenario. Michael had the knowledge of right and wrong in this situation. He fully knew what responsibilities he had and the time that was necessary to complete them. He just didn't want to be responsible for carrying them out. So long as he could get someone else to be his conscience, he could concentrate on pursuing pleasure and avoiding pain.

But by continuing to remind and nag him about his chores, his parents were taking the monkey of Michael's responsibility and putting it on their backs. This monkey was huge, weighing them down, frustrating them greatly. By telling Michael that he had to decide for himself whether or not he had the freedom to go to his friend's house, Carly was putting that monkey back onto Michael where it belonged, forcing him to take ownership of his responsibilities.

Suppose Michael refused to take the monkey back by deciding he could go to his friend's house, after all, neglecting his responsibilities in the process. Carly would then have two options. She could either take the monkey back and continue to lecture, remind, and nag him, or she could give him a consequence. In this case, the consequence would be that he would lose the privilege of going to his friend's house because he didn't complete his tasks on time. But both of these options are less than desirable.

REFLECTIVE SIT-TIME—
TAKING OWNERSHIP OF HEART ISSUES

Transferring ownership of responsible behavior goes far beyond chores, breakfast routines, and schoolbags. Ultimately, you want your children to take ownership of their own heart actions. It is our experience that nothing can speed this process more than what we call *reflective sit-time.*

A reflective sit-time allows the opportunity for the child to sit and think about what he should have done or said. It is a corrective strategy, not a punitive one. It is to help bring a child to repentance, forgiveness, and restoration and help a child morally evaluate his or her circumstance and then take ownership for the present and future responses. Reflective sit-time is a great tool for children six years of age and older.

To demonstrate the power of reflective sit-times, we will offer two scenarios. The first demonstrates what happens when the parent wrongly assumes ownership of heart issues. The second demonstrates what happens when the child is given opportunity to own his or her own heart attitudes and actions. As in the case of all of our examples, both scenarios are true-life stories.

Cindy's Story

"Mom," Cindy said, "will you sign my papers for school?"

"Let me review them," mom said. "Cindy, what is this?"

"It's a paragraph I had to write for school. Will you just sign it, please?"

"You are not turning this in, young lady," mom said. "Cindy, you are eleven years old. Just look at it—this is sloppy work."

"Mom! It doesn't have to be perfect. The teachers don't care what it looks like."

"Well, I care," mom said. Now it's getting ugly. "Cindy, look at me when I'm talking to you. And don't roll your eyes at me, young lady."

"I wasn't rolling my eyes! Mom, you're being unfair."

"Cindy, don't talk to your mother that way. Child, you need an attitude adjustment."

"What are you going to do—send me to my room?"

"Yes, I think I will. Good idea. I am tired of the way you do your work and the way you talk to me. It isn't right. You have no respect for me."

"What did I do?"

"You wrote a sloppy paper and you argued with me. You rolled your eyes at me and talked back to me. That's what you did. What you need to do, young lady, is apologize to me for all these things, and then redo your paper—neatly this time. Whether you believe me or not, the work you hand in at school represents me, too. Frankly, I don't want the teachers thinking I don't care if you do sloppy work. I don't know why I have to keep telling you these things over and over and over again. When will you ever learn, Cindy?"

What do you think? Did the mother do well or poorly in this situation? Unfortunately, this scene reflects an all-too-common parenting style. Cindy's mom took ownership of Cindy's heart and attitude. But it didn't belong to her. With mom doing all the thinking and talking, Cindy really did not have to think at all. Mom was right there telling her. She did not have to morally process the rightness or wrongness of her actions. Mom did it for her. As long as that continues, mom should expect Cindy's poor behavior to continue.

Later in this chapter we will discuss what could have been done differently. For now, let's work through our second scenario, this time using a reflective sit-time.

Whitney's Story

She did it again! Why couldn't she get this? George felt his frustration growing. Six-year-old Whitney was always in too much of a hurry when she got out of the van. She had the bad habit of launching the van door aside and letting it crash on its back hinges. The din of metal on metal was George's reminder that his message, "Open the door carefully," hadn't sunk in yet.

Normally, George would begin with a lecture—unwittingly gathering up all of Whitney's monkeys. "Whitney, you know better. How many times do I have to tell you to slide that door back carefully? I'm tired of telling you. You're going to break the door. You've got to be more careful with Aunt Jenny's van. Do you understand?" With the lecture complete, Whitney then would give a quick, "Sorry, Dad," and be on her way.

But this time George tried a new tactic. Instead of telling Whitney all she did wrong, he calmly directed her to a chair in the living room. "Whitney, I want you to sit here and think about what you did. I'll be back in a few minutes to check on you."

At first Whitney protested. "Dad, I don't know what I did."

"That's why I want you to think about it. And Whitney, you can have nothing in your hands while you're thinking about this problem. Put the couch pillow down."

Ten minutes passed before George returned. He gently asked, "Can you tell Dad what you did wrong?"

"Yes," Whitney said with a contrite tone. "I wasn't careful with Aunt Jenny's van door."

"That's right," George said. He went on to explain in six-year-old language the first principle, especially how it relates to respecting other people's property. George then moved on to the next step. "Now, Whitney, I want you to sit and think about this question: What must you do to make this right? I'll be back in a few minutes."

Whitney pondered the question. Here was where she faced the real test of her moral knowledge. This was the proving ground of parental training. The question is a test for George's parenting as well as a challenge for Whitney's moral processing skills. Had her parents done enough work in heart-training their daughter? Had they sufficiently deposited knowledge in her moral warehouse?

In a few minutes, George returned to find Whitney's eyes cloudy and her heart heavy. She knew her wrong extended back further than just this one episode. George asked, "Whitney, do you know what you must do to make this right?"

"I think so," she said, tears brimming in her eyes. "When Aunt Jenny comes back to town, I need to ask her for forgiveness for not being careful with her car."

George smiled. Whitney had finally gotten it. She had taken moral ownership of her own wrong and the pathway to make it right. She had gotten there without dad. When it happens like this, the lesson sticks. Whitney took care of her own monkey.

Whitney morally processed her own actions, and it became a deposit for the future. And dad learned a lesson in child management as well. He learned that giving Whitney the opportunity to own her own behavior is far better than giving her another lecture. In this case, Whitney's heart did all the lecturing needed.

We are happy to provide an epilogue to Whitney's story. It has been several months now since this real-life episode took place. This little girl truly learned her lesson. Whitney now possesses a wonderful self-owned sensitivity for property belonging to others—especially how to exit a car with care.

Now, let's contrast the difference between the two scenarios. In our first example, Cindy never really took ownership of her behavior. Mom did it for her. Poor Cindy. In truth, she was the victim of mechanical parenting. Any positive impact on her behavior was temporary. Mom did not empower her child to take ownership responsibility of her own mistakes. No moral internalization, no transformation of the heart. Just another lecture.

Whitney's heart, in contrast, was transformed because it was challenged by an inner voice being stirred. The inner voice of her conscience began to speak of right and wrong, carefulness and carelessness. George challenged his daughter to think and morally process, to take ownership. That is exactly what a reflective sit-time will do for your child.

The-Please-and-Thank-Yous

There is a category of behavior we call the please-and-thank-yous of life. These are the moral courtesies you have attempted to instill into your child. Learning to say please, for example, when one wants something is a moral courtesy that every child should learn to extend.

Your four-year-old child comes to you and says, "Mom, can I have some orange juice?" Never mind for a moment that *may I* is always nicer than *can I*. Generally, the typical response of mom would be something like, "What do you say?" or "What are the magic words?" or "How do you ask?" But by asking these questions, mom has taken the monkey from her child. She has excused him from having to take personal ownership for his own manners.

To avoid taking this monkey, mom could respond, "No, I am sorry but you may not have any orange juice" or "No, Mom doesn't have the freedom to give you orange juice right now," or "You need to sit for a minute and think about why you do not have the freedom to have a drink right now." Through this little exercise, the child will take ownership of her own behavior in the future. Remember, if mom is always reminding, the child never has to learn the lesson.

Normally what happens in the scene above is this: the child instantly responds to mom: "May I *please* have some orange juice?" For a four-year-old, mom may decide to go ahead and let the child have the drink. But for an older child (seven years old and up), she may decide additional time might help the learning process. "Honey, in five minutes you can return with your proper request."

When mom asked her child to sit and think in the above scenario, she was using what we call a reflective sit-time. A reflective sit-time allows the opportunity for the child to sit and think about what he should have done or said. It is a corrective strategy, not a punitive one. It is to help bring a child to repentance, forgiveness, and restoration, and to help a child morally process and evaluate his or her actions.

When presenting this concept in seminars, we are commonly asked who determines the length of the sit-time, the child or the parent? The answer depends on the context of the wrong and the child's age. With younger children, parents should monitor the child's readiness to share. In the case of seven-year-old Whitney, George checked in after ten minutes to see how she was doing. For some children, a reflective sit-time might take five minutes. For others, it might take much longer, depending on the complexity of the situation and the moral readiness of the child.

Amy's Story

Briana was celebrating her eleventh birthday, together with her family. They were traveling on her birthday, but her parents brought along many of her gifts. Her special present that year was something she had been wanting for a long time: a vanity for her bedroom. After opening her gifts, Briana's dad told her that a special gift was waiting for her at home, because it was too large to bring along. Briana started giving guesses as to what it might be. Amy, Briana's eight-year-old sister, blurted, "It's a vanity!" Immediately, tears flooded Briana's eyes.

Amy was instructed by her parents to go into another room to sit and think about what she had done and be prepared to give an answer. This was a reflective sit-time. Amy was asked to morally process what had just happened. Her parents were expecting more from her than, "I told Briana what her gift was." They expected her to move to a much deeper level of contemplation.

After forty-five minutes, Amy tearfully confessed what she had done, and her confession was beautiful: "I stole Briana's joy of receiving the gift as a surprise." Wow! Where did that answer come from? From an ability to morally process. Here an eight-year-old child coming up with an adult-sized answer.

The prerequisite to moral reasoning is knowing moral truth. This assumes that mom and dad have been actively investing moral truth into Amy's heart. In Amy's case, they had. From the time she was three and wanted to pick the flowers, they had told her the why of right and wrong. This deposit of moral truth created an infrastructure of logical thought that enabled Amy to deeply process. Without a knowledge of virtues and values, children will be limited in their ability to reason and process moral situations.

After hearing Amy's response, her parents then instructed her to think about what she must do to make it right. She sat alone for an additional thirty minutes before she responded with another profound answer. She came to realize that she could never give Briana back her joy about this gift. What a lesson in life. Her parents agreed, reminding her that she must guard against taking things from others that she can never give back.

How You Know It's Worked

A reflective sit-time has been effective when the answer the child gives comes from the level of the conscience. A satisfactory response has two components: *What I did* (what was wrong, how was it wrong, why it was wrong, who it hurt) and *What I can do to make it right.* If the child comes back with a shallow response, send him back for more time. The next step is to carry out the things he needs to do to make it right.

SUMMARY

Go back and review the conversation between Cindy and her mom. Try to spot the places where mom is taking monkeys back onto herself. Now let's consider how she could have handled the situation differently.

"Mom," Cindy said, "will you sign my papers for school?"

"Why does your teacher want me to sign them?" mom asked.

First, mom needs to know the reason the teacher wants parents of her students to sign homework. Cindy is responsible to supply this information, unless mom has received the information directly from the teacher via a note or personal contact. If, by signing the paper mom is indicating to the teacher that she thinks Cindy's work is acceptable, then mom has assumed part of the responsibility for Cindy's schoolwork.

When working in tandem with a teacher, this is not necessarily wrong for parents to do. In any case, parents should be concerned about the work their children do. Certainly parents can be working with their children to teach them to be neat and orderly, and that this would apply to how they do their chores, dress themselves, and complete their school assignments. All these things considered, just how can Cindy's mom help her accept responsibility for her actions and attitudes?

Mom looked at the paper, then put it down. "Cindy, I'm sorry, but I don't have the freedom to sign this work."

"But it's due today!"

"I understand that. You are certainly free to turn it in, but I cannot sign it."

"But the teacher won't accept it without your signature."

"Cindy, I understand that this puts you in a predicament. But the responsibility for getting your work done neatly and in on time is yours, not mine. Maybe you just need to take a minute and figure what to do about it."

Cindy was well aware of when this assignment was due and how long she would need to complete it. It really didn't matter why the work was not neat. The point was, it was Cindy's obligation to take care of it. Ultimately, Cindy's mom was saying she was willing for Cindy to receive a lower grade. If she shielded Cindy from the consequences of her actions, she was not doing her daughter any favors. And she was taking a monkey back, which didn't do herself any favors, either.

When parents refuse to take ownership of monkeys that rightly belong to their children, it eliminates power struggles. It equips children to think for themselves, to process moral truth in life's varied scenarios, and to take responsibility for their own behavior.

We sometimes wonder what our society would look like if everyone took responsibility for his or her behavior. How much nicer the shopping malls and airports of our world would be. How much emptier our prisons.

You may not be able to change the world, but you can change your little corner of it.

QUESTIONS FOR REVIEW

1. At what point does a child become accountable for specific behaviors?

2. When do behavioral monkeys jump from the child's back to the parents?

3. How do you know when you have picked up too many monkeys?

4. What is the monkey repellent phrase and what does it do?

5. In refusing to take back a specific monkey from a child, what does a parent empower the child to do?

6. What is the prerequisite for moral processing? How does it work?

Chapter Eleven

Encouragement and Correction: One Coin, Two Sides

*D*iscipline. Kids resist it. Parents do or don't give it. Schools crave it. Just what in heaven's name is it? It's probably not what you think. Discipline is a variety pack of essential principles and actions, all designed to put children on the right path and keep them there.

Some of these principles and actions are encouraging and positive. They serve to train the child's heart through affirming good behavior as it blossoms. Other parts are corrective and constraining. These serve to reel the child in, bringing him back into the circle of compliance. Both sides of discipline are necessary for a child to emerge from childhood a well-rounded, fully seasoned human.

Unfortunately, encouragement is something many parents fail to apply to their children, particularly during the first five years. During that time, parents are so preoccupied with getting things under control that they forget to encourage their tender brood.

After all, endless correction is draining—on all of you. Even if something good does happen, often mom is likely to think, "About time." Yet the opportunity to turn this kid around may well rest in that rare moment of goodness.

Take a deep breath, put on a smile, and tell your struggling child he did something good. You might just witness the dawning of a new day. Without that encouragement, your continuously failing youngster remains in a perpetual state of discouragement. "I can't do anything right." Sometimes your silence in moments of goodness does more to discourage him than a day's worth of deserved correction.

Everyone enjoys a pat on the back. "Well done" is like a one-hundred dollar bill when it comes from someone of influence. An old Hebrew proverb says, "Pleasant words are a honeycomb, sweet to the soul and healing to the bones."[12] Everyone appreciates hearing how his actions pleased or helped another.

This is true for our children, too. "You made your bed beautifully! I thought Daddy must have done it." "Thanks for putting away your laundry without me asking. That's very grown-up." Children are delighted when justified praise comes their way. And you can be sure that behavior that receives praise will be repeated. That's the essence of positive, constructive, encouraging discipline.

Even if you have to start small, find something to notice. Get creative. "Thanks for throwing away your tissue in the trash can instead of leaving it like a trophy on your night table." Well, don't get too creative. Be sure your praise is sincere.

Your child's behavior will always fall into one of two categories: moral and amoral (without a moral dimension). Learning to tie a shoelace, ride a bike, kick a ball, climb a rope, play the piano, or butter a bagel are amoral activities. These skills are associated with natural growth and development and not with any moral sense of rightness or wrongness. They are functions of life, not matters of morality. Moral behaviors, on the other hand, are things like obedience, kindness, honesty, respect, honor, and integrity. These are part of a child's moral development.

Parents need to continuously bear in mind whether they're dealing with moral or amoral (morally neutral) behavior. The two types should obviously be treated differently. You teach an amoral skill like jumping rope in a far different way than you teach a moral skill, such as not interrupting conversation. The first focuses on a child's natural abilities; the second on the issues of the heart.

There will be times when a skill activity lapses over into the moral realm. Learning to ride a bike is a skill, but riding a bike recklessly, endangering another child, puts it in the moral realm. Learning to swim is a skill, but dunking other children is wayward behavior. Parents shouldn't treat these equally. Not knowing how to swim is a deficiency in skill; disregarding other children's safety in the water is a deficiency in character. Parental discernment is necessary for judicial decision-making.

ENCOURAGING MORAL BEHAVIOR

Positive reinforcement tools include verbal affirmation, goal incentives, praise, and rewards. We'll look at those first. Later, we'll look at corrective or negative reinforcement tools, which include verbal reproof, natural consequences, isolation, restrictions, and loss of privileges. Each card in the discipline deck has a legitimate place in the overall pack.

Verbal Affirmation

"Jenna, thank you for getting out of the pool to greet Grandma. That was a wonderful show of respect."

"Billy, I noticed how you held the door for your sister when you saw her coming with her arms full. That was so thoughtful."

Every day, in a hundred ways, you have opportunities to affirm your child. Just because you said something yesterday, don't neglect doing it today.

"Thank you for carrying your plate to the sink. That's a help to Mom."

"Samantha, you folded your pajamas so nicely this morning. Great work."

Simple statements? Yes, but packed with power for your precious child.

CHILDWISE PRINCIPLE #13
Verbal affirmation is never redundant.

In healthy relationships, verbal affirmation is never redundant. Kids (and adults alike) have a "gas tank" for affirmation. It needs to be filled early and topped off throughout the day. We may not see it happen, but our words have tremendous impact on our children. We are shaping our children, sculpting them, with the words we cast at and around them.

Some people believe plants do better if they are talked to, sung to, or whatever. Whether that's true or not, it's a useful analogy for our purpose. If we want a tall and beautiful "child-plant," we liberally apply sincere verbal affirmation. A child who does not receive this nourishment will be, in a sense, stunted.

Think about it: When someone comes up to you and says something like, "I appreciate your compassionate spirit," doesn't it make you want to redouble your efforts to make their words even more true? That person cast a vision for you—a vision you liked very much—so you rise to the level of their praise.

On the other hand, let's say someone comes up to you and says, "Are you always that insensitive with people? I bet you don't keep friends for long." Now how do you feel? You may feel like crawling down a hole to hide. What's the point?

If words, positive and negative, have such an effect on a big adult like you, keep in mind what words—your words—do to your small, tender child. Look for things to praise about your child. Catch her doing something right.

Concentrate on behaviors and attitudes, rather than attributes. Saying, "Thank you for remembering to say please," is better than "My, your eyes sure are pretty." The second one isn't wrong, but it's not encouraging a desired behavior. The child can't do anything about her eyes, but she can sure try hard to always remember to say please.

Look for the little things as well as the big. Yes, it's easier to catch their big efforts, but many times it is the daily stuff that makes or breaks future relationships. Sometimes a simple, "Thank you for closing the patio door," can go a long way.

Another way to verbally encourage a child is to say, "I need your help sweeping the porch" instead of, "I want it cleaned" or just, "Do this." The humility it takes to ask for help by expressing your sincere need elevates the other person. It communicates: "You're needed."

Try linking your words of encouragement to your child's efforts. "Ashley, I was proud of the way you greeted Mr. and Mrs. Roderick. You were so polite. I can tell you're really working on that." "Jennifer, I'm listening to you play the piano. I can hear how much you have improved over last week by just adding five minutes more to your practice time." In both illustrations, the praise was tied to gains made as a result of practice. Linking your encouragement to a specific activity encourages the child to continue his efforts.

Chelsea walked over to show her mom the picture she had colored. Mom complimented her neatness: "What a good job of staying in the lines, Chelsea." Children will often share little successes with their parents simply for the purpose of hearing praise. Such confirmation encourages their hearts.

We have found that the most effective praise is that which comes when the child is not expecting it. For example, if Chelsea's mom had come to the table while the girl was still coloring and commented on how well she was staying within the lines, it would have meant even more. Because the praise was unexpected, it will be remembered each time the activity is repeated. Surprise your kids with praise.

Then, there's your touch. So much is communicated by a

touch. It's a language all its own, a parallel message to whatever you say. Simply place a hand on your son's or daughter's shoulder and say, "I was proud of the way you picked up all the toys without being asked." A light touch around the back, atop the child's head, or gently on the hand conveys something of your heart.

"Thank you," you might say, stroking her cheek, "for not losing patience with your little sister." That verbal affirmation/physical touch combination is unbeatable for filling up a child's affirmation tank. It might also work with your spouse.

One caution. Praise, like any good thing, has its limits. Don't overdo it. A child who is routinely praised can come to view the primary purpose for behaving well as earning praise, not living out virtue. The effort becomes hollow and self-serving. First-century Christian leader, Paul of Tarsus, warned that smooth talk and flattery deceive the minds of naive people.[13] That warning is very applicable. Unmerited or exaggerated praise is false flattery and it works against everything you are attempting to achieve.

Use Goal Incentives to Encourage

Parents can use goal incentives to help train a child to ride a bike, color a picture, improve a grade, or learn to type. All of these morally neutral activities are worthy of incentives. However, not all morally neutral activities are skill-related. For example, eating potato chips on the couch is morally neutral, but it has nothing to do with developing a skill.

The Ezzos once lived near a lake. They wanted to "waterproof" their young children by teaching them how to swim. To facilitate Amy's learning, Gary offered her a goal incentive by saying, "Amy, if you learn to swim this summer from the dock to the yellow buoy, we'll buy you the snorkel set you saw in the store."

That summer, she made learning to swim a priority. Her motivation was heightened by the incentive. She worked diligently, learned to swim to the buoy, and received her bright yellow snorkel. If she had not met her goal, she would have received praise for trying, but not the snorkel set.

Goal incentives differ from rewards and bribes. Rewards and bribes are tied to habits of the heart—moral issues—while goal incentives should be used for amoral activities, such as training a child to ride a bike, color a picture, improve a grade, or type. While it might sound like a matter of semantics, there is a discernible difference between the three. Parents use goal incentives to motivate actions associated with skills, talents, and intellectual challenges, but not to change or modify behavior, as is the case with rewards and bribes.

When we use the term *behavior,* we are speaking of moral rightness or wrongness. When we speak of skills and talents, we are speaking of native abilities that have no rightness or wrongness attached to them. Learning how to swim has no moral implications. Being a bully in the water does. Learning to throw a ball is amoral. Throwing a ball to hurt another child is moral—or in this case, immoral.

Later, we will talk about rewards and their negative counterpart, bribes, and how to rightly and wrongly employ them in parenting. For now, it is enough to say that goal incentives can be a great encouragement for a child who needs a little "oomph" to get over a hurdle of doubt. But goal incentives have a limit.

Be careful not to use goal incentives to a child's discouragement. That happens when a parent expects more from the child than is reasonable for his or her age. At four, Amy learned to swim an appropriate distance, but she was not yet ready to swim the length of the lake. She would have failed to achieve the goal *and* the incentive. This would've crushed her desire to attempt difficult things.

Rewarding Behavior

Verbal encouragement will stimulate right behavior, but the purpose of a *reward* is to confirm and reinforce proper behavior. "Ryan, because you behaved so well in the store today, Mom wants to demonstrate her appreciation by letting you pick out a special treat." This is an example of rewarding a child. Mom called attention to his good conduct and showed her appreciation for it. It came *after the fact*—which is what separates a reward from a bribe.

You might wonder, "Okay, but what's the difference between a bribe and a goal incentive?" Bribing takes place when you offer something up front in exchange for good behavior later on. "Jonathan, if you're good in the store today, Mommy will buy you a special treat. But you have to be good." That's a bribe. Yeah, you got the behavior, but at what expense? The child's right behavior did not come out of a desire to do good, but a desire for a temporary gratification.

Bribes pervert all sense of virtue. Children will respond to a bribe, but the changed behavior will last only as long as the bribe has influence. Grandma Bee always bribes little Johnny with a piece of candy just to get him to sit in his chair. But she could never understand why he would not do so on his own. Little Johnny had figured it out. You see, once the pleasure of a bribe is consumed, you are left with a behavioral vacuum.

Goal incentives are also offered up front, not to motivate morally right or wrong behavior, but to help a child achieve a developmental skill. Another distinction between the two is found in the aftereffects. Goal incentives help establish lifelong skills. Once a child learns to swim, tie a shoelace, ride a bike, or play the piano, it becomes part of her life. The bribe is a temporary appeasement with no positive lingering effects.

Here is a handy rule of thumb: Children should be rewarded for their obedience, not obedient for a reward.

Correcting Childish Behavior

In an earlier chapter, we drew a distinction between two kinds of wrong behavior: childishness and defiance. Childishness springs from a lack of knowledge about what was right. Childishness can also be purely accidental. There was no intent to disobey or do harm. Defiance, on the other hand, is simply that: rebellion against what the child knows to be correct.

We turn now to what to do about childishness. If injury has been done to property or person because of an accident, mistake, or uninformed decision, you need to correct the problem. Here are a few suggestions for handling childish mistakes.

Admonishment

Correcting childish behavior begins with admonishment, a verbal warning. Admonishment is a great training word and concept. It means to warn. Admonishment, then, is warning a child that an action is unwise and may bring calamity upon himself or others.

Brian is conscientious and usually parks his bike in the garage when he is finished riding it. But one day, in a rush to share some news with his mom, he dropped his bike in the front yard and ran inside the house. Then he forgot about it. When his father came home, he found the bike in the front yard.

Was Brian wrong for leaving his bike on the front lawn? Yes. Was it done with the motive to disobey? No. It was a childish act—maybe not smart, but certainly not evil. For that rare offense, his dad admonished him to be sure to put the bike in a safe place each time he finished riding. That warning served to encourage Brian to be responsible. If Brian's dad were to find the bicycle in the front yard the next day, Brian would receive something more than an admonishment.

Logical Consequences

Some mistakes bypass the admonition stage and go straight to consequences. The consequences should be logically connected to the child's wrong (logical consequences). If a child abuses the privilege of playing on his computer, parents should not take away his bike privileges. Keep this in mind for applying consequences to defiance, too.

The purpose of consequences is to encourage good management of property, privileges, and personal behavior.

With property. Teaching a child how to be a good steward of his own possessions will help him be responsible with other people's things. Let's return to Brian and his bike.

A couple of days after the first incident, Brian left his bike near the front porch while he dashed into the house for his jacket. Sure, he remembered his dad's warning, but this was different. He wasn't actually leaving the bike there. Mentally, he was still on the bike. His body was just making a pit stop. Then the phone rang and, since it might be his buddy, he grabbed it. Jack told him about this cool snake he found out back in the garden. It was a long snake— and an equally long story. By now, Brian's bike was most certainly parked.

Brian hadn't intended to ignore his father's counsel, but he took an unwise chance, believing he would be in the house for only a moment. When his dad arrived home and found the bike, he was not amused. It didn't matter that Brian had intended to move the bike. What mattered was that it was where it was not supposed to be. He moved to the consequences level: He took the bike away from Brian for a couple of days. It helped Brian learn that part of owning a bicycle is taking care of it.

Explanations should always accompany stewardship training. As your child grows, however, the explanations should get briefer. By the time Brian is nine years old, he already knows his bike could get stolen or rust in bad weather if left out. Dad doesn't need to go into these in-depth. "Brian, in your hurry, you're forgetting that your bike could be taken or ruined if left outside. To help remind you, I'll hang on to it for two days." That's it.

With privileges. Consequences can also help a child learn to be responsible with a privilege. For example, Cheryl asked if she could feed peanuts to the blue jays. Her mom gave a qualified yes. She gave Cheryl instructions to break the shells on the grass and not on the patio like she had done last time. When Cheryl's mom found her standing on the patio with shells underfoot, she applied a consequence: Since Cheryl had not exercised responsible behavior according to the instructions given, her mother denied her the privilege of feeding the blue jays for a couple of weeks. Cheryl was also responsible for cleaning up her mess.

For young children, even something as simple as retrieving the mail, filling the puppy's water bowl, or taking cookies to the elderly couple across the street are privileges. Once they understand that such privileges may be taken away, children take great pleasure in proving themselves reliable and worthy.

With personal responsibility. If a child's accidental or nonmalicious actions affect people or property, she should nevertheless be held personally responsible. Do you remember the hide-and-seek example? Although Nate didn't mean to knock over the lamp, he was still held responsible for the mistake. Damage was done, unintentional though it was.

The goal of parenting is to cause a child to internalize the responsibility for moral behavior. In a sense, parents are "installing" a conscience. Even in the case of accidents, children must be taught to take ownership for wrongs done. The consequences leveled on Nate (extra chores to make money for restitution) were not punishment, but teaching aids in this process.

CORRECTING DEFIANT BEHAVIOR

There are few areas in parenting that attract more heated debate or controversy than this portion of discipline—correcting willful defiance. Some parents have difficulty accepting the idea that their children can do anything intentionally wrong. They assume that if a child misbehaves, he does so either because they, the parents, have failed to understand the child's needs or because such behavior is a normal part of the child's development, and will eventually be outgrown.

The evidence suggests that children not only have the capacity to do harm, but actually choose to do so with regularity. "Danny, don't touch that. It's hot." *One thousand one, one thousand two.* "Waaaaaa!" Willful disobedience must be corrected. Not only did little Danny suffer the natural consequences of his defiance, his parents ought to consider whether additional punitive measures would be appropriate to correct his diminutive revolution.

All rebellious behavior needs correction, but, as we discussed in an earlier chapter, parents shouldn't correct all rebellion the same way or with the same strength of consequence. Since offenses range from infrequent and minor infractions to serious and repeated defiance, correction should reflect the degree of the offense. Generally speaking, a child's defiance could be categorized at one of three levels:

- serious offenses that require the full weight of the law;
- infractions that need some action and which call for more than a verbal reprimand;
- minor infractions that call only for verbal correction.

In the early years, level one is used more than levels two or three. At this stage, parents are setting up the major boundaries of acceptable behavior. They are simple and absolute. As the child matures, she is more able to grasp the concept of right and wrong, and will need less drastic corrections (most of the time).

Level 1: Crime and Punishment

The top level of offense refers to the worst kinds of disobedience: open defiance, intentional injury, and malicious property damage. Believe it or not, all children (and adults) are capable of this level of trespass. We see examples of each all around us: the "NO!" in the toy store, the new kid pushed off the monkey bars, and the dismembered Barbie on the living room floor.

This level of offense requires parents to bring the whole set of correction skills to bear. Natural and logical consequences, loss of privileges, isolation, sit time—and for some, a swat—are all various methods used at level one.

Spanking. Before going any further we wish to address the issue of spanking. If correctional discipline is the most combustible aspect of parenting, spanking is the flashpoint. In recent years, child-rearing experts have spoken out strenuously on spanking—both in favor of and in opposition to it.

Some opponents of spanking seem to view any form of spanking as abusive. But any form of discipline taken to an extreme or carried out in anger is potentially abusive. Under the right (or rather, the wrong) circumstances, time-outs could be abusive. Mom's frustrated screaming frenzy has got to be considered abusive to a child. Do not kid yourself: You must control yourself before you can control your child.

Opponents equate spanking with hitting, violence, cruelty,

aggression, assault, lashing, beating, and whipping. Is a mother who swats her three-year-old on the behind for running toward a busy street really guilty of child abuse?

If spanking is child abuse, then eating is gluttony. Some who eat are gluttons, but not all. Some who spank are abusers, but not all.

Statistically, the majority of American parents (70 to 90 percent, depending on which report you read) see spanking as a legitimate form of correction. Prospanking statistics do not necessarily prove the practice right or wrong, but they do reflect the feelings of the majority and a deep-seated cultural belief in the curbing benefits of spanking.

Childwise will not address spanking as a disciplinary method. This decision should not be construed as a recommendation to spank or not to spank. It is simply a recognition of the complexity associated with the method. We encourage parents who choose to employ corporal punishment to realize that it is not a fix-all solution and should never be done with anger or with the intent of getting even with the child. Spanking is a private matter between parent and child and should be offered with love and within limits.[14]

Whatever form of correction you use, you know it's worked when your child's demeanor softens and she seeks to be close with you once it's over. In fact that is one of the signs of true repentance. A desire to restore the relationship is a healthy sign that the heart has been cleaned out and the child is seeking to restore the relationship with the one offended. Often it is with the parent.

Natural consequences. Sometimes defiance produces its own pain. For example, Melissa's mother instructed her to stop running on the sidewalk because of the danger of tripping on the big cracks in the cement. Melissa chose to disregard mom's instructions, resulting in scraped and bruised knees. Instantly, Melissa's mother had her teaching tool. This is what we call "natural consequences." Natural consequences can be extremely effective in correcting defiant behavior, but can also help a child accept responsibility for his own time management.

For example, your child loves to go to nursery school but is never ready on time. This sends the stress level in your house through the roof every morning, and you are forced to rush him to school. Here is our recommendation. If nursery school starts at 9:00 A.M. and it takes ten minutes to get there, do not say to the child, "If you're not ready to go by 8:50 A.M., you will not go to school today." That deadline only puts more pressure on *you* because you are left in a state of tension wondering whether he is going to make it or not. Set the child's deadline for 8:30 A.M. If he is not ready by that time, he loses the privilege of going.

With this earlier deadline, you are not stressed out, wondering if you are going to make it on time. You can warn the child at 8:25 A.M. that he has five minutes left, but if he chooses by his actions to present himself ready at 8:35 A.M., the privilege of going to school should be withdrawn. Do not be a softy and go back on your established deadline, even if he shows up at 8:31 A.M. Children quickly develop contempt for wishy-washy authority. The child needs to learn that some things in life are very exact. An exception, however, occurs when a child is characterized by being ready on time but is late once. Withholding a privilege in this case would not be appropriate.

Logical consequences. When there are no natural consequences to a wrong act, parents can employ logical consequences. By definition a logical consequence is a form of correction that is logically connected to a wrongful act. For example, if your child abuses the privilege of playing on his computer, don't take away his television privileges or his bike. There is no logical connection back to his computer offense with those restrictions. A logical alternative is to shut the computer down for a couple of days. Losing his keyboard privileges will drive the lesson home faster than anything else.

One final word about the use of natural and logical consequence. Make sure the child and not the parent is being punished. If you take away TV privileges at a time you customarily go into another room to read the paper, whom have you really punished? Try to avoid punishing the innocent while correcting the guilty. The rest of the family should not be held hostage to one child's time of correction.

Isolation. Isolation is another discipline tool. It works because children are social beings. Isolation means temporarily taking away the privilege of social contact. For example, when one child becomes continually disruptive in group play, one option is to remove him to play by himself or not play at all. He might be sent to his room to contemplate his antisocial behavior. It is the pain of removal that carries the impact. In some cases playtime may not be over, but the privilege of playing with others' kids might be.

Isolation should be reserved for drawing attention to the more serious offenses. Even so, it is not an end-all to discipline. Like other tools in the disciplining parent's bag, it can be very effective when used appropriately—and ineffective when misused. Isolation as a structured consequence can begin with a child as young as nine months of age and can be used through the middle years.

Level 2: Beyond Verbal Admonishment

Level two offenses are those that are not nearly as serious as to require the full force of parental action, but which call for more than a simple spoken reprimand. Level two offenses include new misbehaviors that are becoming more common, old habits that are reemerging, or yesterday's warning that has not been heeded.

There are a variety of possible consequences a parent may apply at level two, but one which is helpful is the use of reflective sit-time (which we discussed in further detail in chapter 10).

A reflective sit-time can serve three purposes. First, it is a *preventative strategy* used to control physical or emotional energy. This is when a child needs to stop, sit down, and get control. Reflective sit-times can be used as a *maintenance strategy* to help a child realign his thinking, and gain self-control over current or potential wrong behavior and move toward wise behavior. Third, a reflective sit-time can be used as a *corrective strategy* assisting a parent in bringing a child to a deeper understanding of his actions and to help facilitate true repentance.

Here is an example of how a reflective sit-time might be used to correct a level two offense. Becky, Brian, and Nathan were playing kickball in the backyard. Their mom approached them and gave the children a warning to be cautious and not kick the ball into the newly planted garden.

While observing from the kitchen window, mom noticed

Becky's lack of caution, as evidenced by the number of times the ball made it to the edge of the garden before being stopped. Before Becky got herself into serious trouble, mom assigned her to a patio chair for five minutes. This was not a punishment, but a time-out designed to help her settle down and gain self-control before she got herself into trouble.

Becky's careless kicking was defiance because she was ignoring her mother's warning. Although the ball never actually made it into the garden, it was clear that Becky was not being cautious. Her offense called for more than a warning (since that hadn't been heeded) but less than a level one consequence.

A reflective sit-time forces the child to stop what he is doing and think. He is instructed to sit, not as a punishment, but as a time to get control of his thoughts and actions and to think about the course he is on before it leads to greater consequences. The idea is to get the child to ask himself, "Do I really want to go in this direction?" If the child emerges from sit-time and continues the defiance, he has automatically qualified himself for a level one consequence.

Reflective sit-times are not the same thing as the "time-outs" often used in our culture. A time-out is not an effective consequence for a repeated offense. Contrary to popular opinion, using time-outs as a primary method of punishment is one of the least effective types of consequence. Here's why.

In a simple penalty box time-out, the child seldom associates sitting in a chair with the act for which he is being punished. That is because the frustration of the parent is usually more prominent in the situation than the act itself. As a result, the child tends to associate time-outs with parental frustration rather than with the wrong behavior. The child is not sitting in a chair contemplating the benefits of a virtuous life, nor is he beating his chest and chanting, "Oh, what a wayward child I am." He's just sitting there waiting for mom to cool off. His future behavior has not been affected in the least.

Level 3: Verbal Admonishment

Level three is the mildest form of correction. It is the equivalent of a minor course correction as you stay in the center of your lane on the highway. In terms of parenting, level three usually takes the form of a spoken warning.

Warnings are appropriate when a child commits a minor offense that she's never committed before. It would be unfair and exasperating to a child to punish her for a single infraction if she is normally characterized by compliance. Admonishment is the proper consequence in this context.

A verbal admonishment usually takes the form of stern words intended to instruct the child that the behavior is wrong and should not be repeated. This is the time to explain, in an eye-to-eye, heart-to-heart manner, why the infraction is wrong.

Your child may want to ask questions. Remember, she's trying to fit all this into her developing framework of right and wrong. She may ask great, penetrating questions, perhaps even revealing inconsistencies in things you've told her. Take the time to dialogue with your child and help her understand how to do what she secretly desires to do: please you.

If, after such a warning, your child repeats the offense, you move up the correction scale.

SUMMARY

Encouragement and correction are two sides of the same coin. Both need to be moderated by love, patience, and parental resolve. Most importantly, both require consistency in application. The more consistent the discipline the happier the child.

A child who receives consistent reinforcement at home will actually be a better student at school. He will learn faster because he possesses a greater ability to integrate and morally process. Always strive for consistency in your parenting!

QUESTIONS FOR REVIEW

1. Describe the difference between moral and amoral behaviors.

2. From this chapter, list the three primary ways to encourage behavior.

3. Explain the difference between childishness and defiance.

4. Cite the difference between a goal incentive and a bribe.

5. When and in what fashion is it acceptable to reward a child for good behavior?

6. When correcting foolish behavior, what are the three levels of offenses to consider?

7. What three purposes can a reflective sit-time serve?

Chapter Twelve

Common Discipline Issues

Some days you seem to have it all. Right out of the starting block, your child's first wakeful moments bring forth a whine, and from there it is all downhill. From a power struggle over putting on shoes to an angry outburst when her closet doors jam, the day seems destined for trials and tragedies.

Early childhood draws a wagonload of such disruptive behaviors. Most parents have at least some personal experience with their children's whining, power struggles, tantrums, lying, stealing, and cheating.

Understand this from the outset: Children engage in such conduct if they find it works to achieve their immediate goal. If a child tries a tantrum, for example, and it gets stopped, he will look for other ways to meet his objectives. But if he throws a fit and the parent gives in, the tantrum tactic is reinforced—and will be repeated. The parent usually walks away from the encounter thinking she's just got a bratty (or "temperamental") child, never realizing that it was her failure to stop the tantrum that caused her child to adopt the habit.

We all want something. Every day, there are things we want to attain, whether it's a raise, a pat on the back, or a few uninterrupted moments. And we all use different tactics to get what we want. Throughout life, we've been trying out different techniques, keeping what works and tossing the rest. Much of this evaluation process is done in childhood.

As a parent, you need to realize the power you hold over which tactics your child will keep in his quiver. Encourage positive ways of pursuing desires; discourage negative ones. Now let's look carefully at some of the more challenging negative tactics to watch out for.

WHINING

You have instructed your four-year-old to try to make her bed. But she doesn't want to. Each morning for a week you hear high-pitched squeals as she struggles with compliance. "I can't." "It's too hard." "Don't like this." "Doesn't look good." If it weren't disobedience, it would almost be comical.

Here is the good news about whining: It can be controlled. It is not a signal of some deep-seated, emotional problem. It is a learned tactic. There is a very good reason why children whine: it works. Persistent whining can wear down the best of mothers. Mom may even become frustrated enough to give in and make the bed herself—but not frustrated enough to correct the behavior. There is hope for the parent of a whiner.

We introduced the "Yes, mom" and "Yes, dad" tool in a previous chapter. This simple little device has proven highly successful in eliminating whining. For example, a mother may respond to whining with the following dialogue: "Nathan, let's get control of your whining. I want you to say: 'Yes, Mom, no whining.'" The child responds, "Yes, Mom, no whining." The child hears himself verbally agree to stop whining. Children usually will not violate what they hear themselves agree to doing. It really is that simple.

Occasionally, a short period of time is needed for the child to readjust to communicating correctly. You may need to tell your child to wait two minutes, then ask mommy again for a drink of water. This allows your child a few moments to consider the consequences of whining and then make a new and dignified start.

TEMPER TANTRUMS

Most three- to seven-year-olds should be beyond the temper tantrum phase. However, if that tactic has been unintentionally strengthened by parents, it may be in full force.

You cannot expect that a child will achieve maturity in emotional behavior any sooner than he will achieve maturity in other areas of development. How he controls and expresses his emotions is far more important than the fact that he merely controls or expresses himself. The first is a learned state, the second is the natural state. There are right ways to express feelings and wrong ways. Throwing temper tantrums is the wrong way.

The propensity for throwing temper tantrums is a normal phase of development. That is not to say temper tantrums must be. Tantrums are triggered by one thing—disappointment. A temper tantrum, whether thrown by a child or an adult, is a coping mechanism occurring because a child has not learned how to correctly manage disappointment. As future control over this emotion increases, the potential for tantrums decreases. Meanwhile, you still need to deal with it. Here are some suggestions.

1. Take note of when and where your child throws his fits. Is it only in public, just before or after a meal, or when he is tired and in need of a nap? If a pattern exists, knowing it will help you prevent tantrums before they happen.

2. As difficult as it may be, try not to talk a child out of his tantrum. Without realizing it, you are encouraging the behavior by rewarding it with attention and gentle words. To work effectively, a tantrum needs a sympathetic audience. Talking provides that audience. Speaking beseechingly to a child in a tantrum is like granting a terrorist's demands.

3. Use isolation against temper tantrums. Deposit the child in his room or on the couch until he settles down. That may take ten minutes or longer. What about the child who will destroy his room during one of his fits? To frankly state our opinion, any child between the ages of three and seven who trashes his room during a time of correction is outwardly displaying total contempt for his parents' right to lead and rule his little life. This can be corrected, but only in time.

4. One technique that some have found helpful in such cases is to physically hold the child. Sit down and hold that child until you feel the struggling arms and flailing legs surrender to your will. Don't let go. When he surrenders, the tantrum is over. And you will see a more peaceful child.

5. Do not add the question "Okay?" to the end of your instruc-

tions. "Johnny, we're going to leave the store now, okay?" This is begging for trouble. What if it is not okay with Johnny? Try it this way: "Johnny, we're going to be leaving the store soon. I want to hear a 'Yes, Mommy.'" A child will not say "Yes, Mommy," and then throw a tantrum.

6. Teach delayed gratification. This must become a reality in your child's life. He simply cannot have everything he wants when he wants it. Immediate gratification training only heightens a child's anxiety when the pattern is not maintained.

FRUSTRATION TANTRUMS

Frustration tantrums are not the same as temper tantrums. A frustration tantrum happens when a child cannot make his body accomplish the task his mind can clearly understand. For example, when Martha tried to place her dolls in a circle, one kept toppling over. She knew in her mind what she wanted to do but could not physically make it happen. Frustration is the basis of these tantrums, not rebellion.

You will naturally desire to help your child when he gets frustrated. You see him in distress and rush to intervene. However, do not be too quick to jump in. You may be encouraging a short temper and a quickness to give up.

Make yourself available but first insist that the child ask for your help. A simple statement such as, "Mom will help you if you want, but you must ask me," puts the burden of cooperative problem solving on the child. This is a virtue to develop in him, because he will need to know how to work with others to solve problems later in life.

If you sense a growing frustration and there is no hope of resolving it, then consider playtime over for now.

POWER STRUGGLES

A power struggle results when parents fail to exercise their authority wisely. That is, they allow themselves to be forced into a "must win" situation over a seemingly minor conflict. There will be some early parent/child conflicts in which parental resolve must be victorious, but you should choose well which hill you're willing to die on. Wise parenting is superior to power parenting.

CHILDWISE PRINCIPLE #14
Wise parenting is better than power parenting.

Surrendering with Dignity

The moment arrives. Your less-than-social son, Stevie, has chosen this occasion to humiliate your entire family by not acknowledging the birthday gift he's just received from Aunt Dee. You're certain that a reminder is all that's needed to defuse the situation, but you're wrong. Little Stevie just stares back at you blankly. Bent on saving face, you tell Stevie, more firmly this time, to look at Aunt Dee and thank her. Stevie simply looks down.

Now what? Unless you've just started speaking Mandarin, Stevie has understood you perfectly. This is a power struggle, make no mistake.

There is a way to defuse such potential power struggles and maintain the integrity of your authority. After the second instruction, you should humbly apologize on behalf of the child. "Aunt Dee, I'm sorry Stevie did not respond appropriately. We're working on this aspect of his character." Then you should direct stubborn Stevie to his room for some well-needed think time. Voilà! The power struggle is unplugged and you have retained your authority.

Stevie may rejoin the party when he is ready to conduct himself appropriately (and thank Aunt Dee).

Children should be allowed the freedom to surrender with dignity. A child will often defy a parent when the parent makes the option of surrender intolerable. That is, a child will persist with wrong behavior if a parent does not give him room to surrender with dignity.

When Stevie's mom battled him toe-to-toe, her direct insistence made surrendering to her authority in front of everyone difficult, if not impossible. Another response would be if she had walked away from the table after her first verbal reprimand to refresh her coffee, Stevie most likely would have come forth with an expression of thankfulness to his aunt. Mom's presence, however, extended the conflict.

By stepping away, mom would have given Stevie room to surrender with dignity rather than face a continued challenge. If Stevie still chose not to properly respond, then removing him would have been the best option. Wise parenting is better than power parenting.

DISHONESTY

Both extremes of parenting—authoritarian and permissive—produce children who tend to lie. Parents who raise their children with overly strict discipline, in which spanking is the answer for everything, will find that their children attempt to escape the inevitable punishment by lying.

Children raised in child-centered homes, in which the child has at least as much voice in the family as the parents, find dishonesty useful too. These children are not looking for escapes from punishment (since punishment rarely occurs), but for ways to gain even more power and to manipulate those blocking their goals. They calculate their dishonesty and attempt to deceive others in hopes of gaining an advantage for themselves.

But lying isn't the only part of dishonesty. We will look at three subdivisions: lying, stealing, and cheating.

Lying—The Ultimate Family Transgression

Dishonesty, as we have said, is more than simply lying. However, lying is probably the most common manifestation of dishonesty. Deception within a family weakens the chain of trust linking each member. Weaken one link and you weaken them all.

What should you do when your child lies? In evaluating how you ought to correct a lie, consider the child's age, his motive for lying, and the characterization of his behavior.

Consider the child's age. The lie of a five-year-old is different from the lie of a ten-year-old. The younger the child, the more shallow will be his moral understanding. The five-year-old does not understand how his lie impacts his relationship with mom, dad, or siblings. An older child, however, is more advanced in his understanding of close relationships. The older the child, the more seriously the lie should be treated.

Lying by an older child can be a sign of serious trouble. It may indicate a growing contempt for you and the people around him. If he doesn't mind lying to you, how do you think he's behaving when he's not with you? In such cases, punishment sometimes can bring a child to regret the lie, but hardly ever causes actual repentance. To eliminate this behavior, parents must chip away at the relational level.

Consider the child's motive. Many times parents can unintentionally become the cause of their child's lie. Listed below are nine basic reasons for lying. We're not trying to excuse prevarication, but only to help you understand why your child may do it. Kids sometimes lie:

- to get attention;
- to gain control over an object or relationship;
- to get revenge;
- to escape responsibility;
- to get accepted;
- to balance out the parents' unfairness;
- because of parental example;
- to gain something (a privilege, activity, or opportunity);
- to avoid losing something (a privilege, activity, or opportunity).

If a child is lying to gain revenge, it is because she feels she has been wronged and the powers that be have not adequately countered the wrong. She needs to learn how to let mom or dad handle the fairness or unfairness of the situation.

If a child seems to be lying to gain your acceptance (or in order to not lose it), examine your parenting practices. Are you placing the bar of "making Mommy happy" too high for your child to reach? Do you hear yourself praising him by saying, "Good boy," instead of "Good work"? If he's a good boy—if his whole self is judged worthwhile and affirmed—when he behaves, what is he when he misbehaves? No wonder he doesn't want to admit doing wrong. Also look for ways you or his siblings might be communicating disapproval.

Go through these nine motives, add to the list as you think of others, and honestly evaluate the possibility that you may be indirectly causing your child to be dishonest. This will give you a starting point toward correcting this wrong behavior.

Consider the characterization of behavior. There is a difference between the child who habitually lies and the one who does so in a moment of weakness. The one who is characterized by lying may be declaring his opinion that relationships mean very little. That child is consumed with self-interest and is not capable of rightly relating to others. For him, lying is a way of life, so honesty is not a value worth upholding. For other children, lying might be a way of coping with abusive parents. It becomes a way of life also, but only for survival.

The child who is not characterized by lying should not receive the same punishment as the one who is. However, both children should receive an explanation of the importance of honesty, trust, and family loyalty. The consequence a parent should apply must be in light of the rarity of the offense.

Also remember the principle of substitution over suppression discussed in chapter 7. Trying to suppress lying is only half a gain. Instilling a sense of honest behavior is the other. Don't forget to elevate the virtue over the vice.

Stealing

Stealing should be treated according to the seriousness of the theft. Taking a cookie from the jar without permission should bring a different punishment from stealing one hundred dollars from dad's wallet. The punishment should fit the crime.

Maybe you remember your own indiscretion at a tender age, when for the overwhelming desire to possess that pack of gum, perfume sampler, or ballpoint pen; something that came home from the store which wasn't yours to keep. Maybe it belonged at the neighbor's house or maybe even in mom's extra freezer where she packs away cookies for Christmas.

When this happens with your child, first consider the context of his thievery. Two children may steal items of similar value, but for one the wrong may be a much more serious offense. Stealing a cookie from the jar is different than stealing a cookie from a bakery. Stealing within the family shames the child; stealing outside the family shames the family.

The best medicine for theft is restitution. It is an excellent way to heighten a child's respect for the property of others. Remember, restitution should be more than 1:1 for stealing. We recommend a 3:1 exchange rate.

A theft is not always tangible. We can steal someone's time as well as stealing their wallet. We've seen a case of stolen joy over a spoiled surprise. But the most treacherous way to rob another human being is to steal his good reputation. Gossip—whether it's in the classroom or the board room—destroys reputations, and these can never be completely restored, no matter what. Teach your children to mind their own business and not be quick to involve themselves in the scandals of others. Slanderous gossip is shattering.

Cheating

Cheating is an act of deceit. Some say cheating only hurts the cheater, but we say cheating affects others, too. Parents should loathe a child's attempts to take advantage of another by cheating.

Children learn how to cheat at an early age. Unfortunately, they often learn it from their parents. How morally credible can a parent be who says to his child, "Tell them you are only twelve so they'll let you in free"? Not very.

Do you sometimes let your child cheat at games, hoping he will find pleasure in victory? "Honey, you moved your piece four spaces but you only rolled two on the dice." "No, Mommy, I rolled four." "Oh, okay."

If your little guy only rolled a two on the dice, don't encourage his deception. By letting him move four spaces in an effort to enhance his confidence, you're actually sending the message that winning is essential to a good self-esteem—and cheating is an acceptable way to win. It is backwards thinking to assume a child will feel good about winning a game through cheating. If he can't handle losing at a board game, he probably isn't old enough to play it.

Teach integrity, not cheating.

SUMMARY

Some parents see it as their duty to make their children happy, never recognizing that this treatment may deprive their little ones of the strength that comes from wise restrictions and loving corrections. These parents give minimal guidance and may even consider guidance to be an intrusion into the child's personality. They bend over backward to allow the child self-expression, regardless of any offensiveness. They avoid correction or calling a child's errors to his attention so as to not give the child an inferiority complex.

Unfortunately, this kind of parenting produces brittle, selfish children who cannot cope with the real world. Parents are supposed to equip their children to handle adult life, not send them out expecting to always be successful, to always get their way, and to never be denied a single desire.

Only when children are sure that their parents care about their actions can they feel desirous of following their parents' lead. Parental restrictions and correction help children "toughen up" and show them the way to live morally. Children need help in knowing what is good for them. Loving restrictions and consistent correction are ways of communicating concretely to the child that he or she is loved.

QUESTIONS FOR REVIEW

1. What type of training actually encourages the misbehavior cited in this chapter?

2. What kind of response from your child will help curb whining? Explain why it works.

3. How can frustration tantrums be defused?

4. What is a power struggle?

5. What does it mean to allow a child to surrender with dignity?

6. Name the three subdivisions of dishonesty.

7. What three things are important to bear in mind when determining consequences for lying?

Chapter Thirteen

Some Nifty Things

Sometimes you need something extra. Even Mary Poppins, with all her charm, nevertheless relied upon a spoonful of sugar to help the medicine go down. And while we cannot promise you toys which march themselves to their box, we do have a few nifty tricks of our own.

Bearing in mind that every child is unique, often requiring an added measure of effort in specific areas, we offer the following ideas to boost positive, controlled training in the life of your child. These ideas work to make life for you, the parent, a bit less turbulent.

QUIETING THE WIGGLES

Do you have one? You know: a mover and a shaker, a high energy, perpetual motion, chase-his-own-tail kid. How many times have you tried to slow your little missile? "Calm down." "Settle down." "Sit still." "Stop moving." "Stop kicking." "Put your hands down." "Sit on your hands." "Be still for a moment." Has it ever worked for longer than a millisecond?

Have you ever thought about what "settle down" or "slow down" looks like to a three-year-old? These are abstract concepts, metaphors. A three-year-old doesn't have a clue what you mean.

The call came in a moment of desperation. "Jessie, I'm getting a little apprehensive about our breakfast meeting with the Ezzos this Saturday. My two little ones do not do well sitting for long periods of time. Help!"

"Louise," Jessie said, "there is a nifty little thing that helps children gain self-control in moments when you most want it and they most need it. Are you ready?"

"Yes!"

"When you begin to see those early signs that your kids are going to lose it, physically or verbally, instruct them to fold their hands and work on getting some self-control."

Louise began the training immediately. She and her family did meet the Ezzos that day for breakfast. Toward the end of the meal, a little wandering leg popped itself up on sister's chair. That would normally be enough of a catalyst to energize the two-and-a-half-year-old and a four-year-old into all-out playtime, right there in the restaurant—but mom had another plan.

Instead of all the classic begs, bribes, and threats, she simply said: "Girls, we're not quite ready to go yet. I want you to fold your hands and get some self-control."

Would you believe those two little girls sat still, with their hands folded in their laps? In less than a minute, they had subdued their impulsive behavior. Without a war of words with mom.

Afterwards, mom pulled out some crayons and let them color on the paper napkins.

Teach your child that self-control begins with the folding of her hands. That is a wonderfully concrete way for her to understand calmness. Her eyes gaze on those peaceful hands lying still in her lap, and soon physical and verbal self-control is achieved.

Why does it work? Because a child's body is full of energy. The energy must go somewhere. When mom says, "Settle down" or "Sit still" or "Stop kicking," nothing happens because she did not redirect the energy. When mom says, "Honey, I want you to fold your hands and get some self-control," now the energy is directed right to those folded hands. Yes, it is that simple.

Have you ever experienced a verbal war in the backseat during a drive to grandma's house? Try this: "Kids, neither one of you is speaking kindly. For a few minutes we are not going to talk. I want you to fold your hands and get some verbal self-control." (Don't forget to get a "Yes, mom.") Why does it work? Verbal energy needs to go somewhere, too. It goes to the hands.

How about a three-year-old throwing a fit in his booster chair because his food is not coming fast enough? Try having him fold his hands and look at them. This nifty trick also helps facilitate patience.

CHILDWISE PRINCIPLE #15
An ounce of self-control is better than a pound of trouble.

Parents should always try to help a child gain self-control *before* the child crosses the bridge of trouble, not afterward. The hand-folding exercise does exactly that. It is a wonderful tool that can be used at checkout counters, school functions, swim lines, dentist's offices, or during that longer-than-usual sermon.

Hand-folding handles all the excessive body energy that makes self-control so difficult. After all, if you want your child to settle down, that energy has to go somewhere. Now, instead of it going into squabbling or cartwheeling or whispering, it can go into the hands.

Another amazing thing about hand-folding is how quickly it brings about self-control. Usually only thirty to ninety seconds need to elapse before mom can say, "Okay, kids, you can let go of your hands." Your child only needs to fold her hands long enough to gain self-control in the moment. Once that is accomplished, mom can redirect the child's energy to productive activities (like coloring on paper napkins).

It is important to teach this technique when things are calm. If you're already in the conflict, your children are not going to be especially attentive pupils. You may have your child practice this at the table while you finish up last-minute mealtime preparations. Make it a fun game in the beginning. Demonstrate how to achieve self-control in a peaceful time, so that when things begin to get out of hand, you've got the cure in place.

This simple technique will become second nature to your child and will work wonders in creating the peace your family deserves.

SLOW, SLOWER, AND SLOWEST—TEACHING THE THREE CANDY SPEED

Your little guy's dentist appointment is in just a few minutes. You completely forgot about it last month, so you want to redeem yourself this time. All you've got to do is have your son pick up his markers and put away his paper. You instruct him to do so. He gives you a nice, "Yes, Mommy," and begins to clean up.

But for some reason you feel like you've entered the Twilight Zone. Right before your eyes, your son, who normally has all the energy in the world, all of a sudden goes limp on you. He moves slower than the 1950's movie *The Blob*.

"Sammy, you have to pick up your crayons right now."

One marker. Pause. Another marker. Yawn.

"Come on, Sammy. Now! I mean it. We have to get going."

One marker. Pause. Another marker. Scratch.

"Sammy, move faster! Sammy, we're going to be late because of you. Come on, Sammy, move faster!"

For mom, this whole episode has transformed into a slow motion dream. Each of the boy's limbs seems attached to an invisible, stretchy web, pulling against him as he reaches for the purple cap.

What's happening here? Clearly, he sees your rush to get out of the house. You prompt him, reminding him to hurry so together you don't steal the dentist's time by being late. You find yourself rambling on with insignificant, energy-draining adult reasoning until you are ready to scream. So, instead, you clean the coffee pot, stick some glasses in the dishwasher, nervously glancing over your shoulder at the clock, then the boy—this strange new glue boy—to check his progress. You know he can move faster. But how do you get him to pick up the pace without sounding like a slave master?

The problem is your child doesn't know what "fast" looks like. It's too abstract. Three candy speed is a way to show him what accelerated movement is.

Surely if your child's favorite candy waited at the end of his task you'd see mercury instead of molasses. But we're not talking about bribery.

Try this sometime when you're not rushed. Begin with a slight mess that your child is able to pick up. Put three little candies on the counter and call your child over. Tell him you are going to set the timer and that he may begin cleaning up when you do so. Inform him that if the toys are picked up and neatly put away, these three candies will be his reward.

At this point, his energy is on full alert and he takes his mark. Go! The child moves faster than you've ever seen, thus beating the timer. This is his three candy speed. You just established in concrete form a time benchmark that becomes a future reference point.

As Sammy's consuming the candy (and before the sugar rush kicks in), sit him down and explain to him that the speed he just moved is called three candy speed. He will not get candy every time. In fact, this is the only time he will get candy for moving fast. Tell him you just wanted him to feel himself going fast so that later, when you need him to move quickly, you can just tell him to go at three candy speed, and he'll know what that feels like.

The next time you need to get moving lickety-split, all you have to do is tell him to pick up his toys in "three candy speed."

READ AFTER DINNER

Have you ever read the true life adventures of Dr. Walter Reed and how he discovered yellow fever? What about Booker T. Washington, friend of presidents, kings, and crowned heads of Europe, who rose from poverty to university president? Have you read about Albert Schweitzer and his great work in Africa? What about Florence Nightingale, Clara Barton, Louis Pasteur, or George Washington Carver?

These are more than legends from our past. They are great men and women of history whose life stories are packed with examples of courage, perseverance, integrity, hard work, and honesty.

All children love stories. After dinner each night, before the dishes were cleared from the table, Anne Marie led the Ezzo family in a story time. It became one of their favorite family memories.

Reading is such a great way to help advance character in children. It is also one of the most pleasant activities that can be shared by all ages. Reading, unlike watching a video, forces their imagination to work, their minds to think, and their hearts to ponder.

Reading is a great means of moral education. Children benefit from the inventory of examples true life stories provide. They learn right and wrong, good and bad, and consequences of each. As Bill Bennett suggests in the *Book of Virtues* (Simon & Schuster),

"Nothing in recent years, on television or anywhere else, has improved on a good story that begins 'Once upon a time.'"[15]

Reading together after dinner did more than add to our minds. It was during times like these that we really gave our children what they needed: a sense of family identity built upon the memories of our togetherness. Pick up a book and start reading as a family after dinner.

CHEERFUL CHORE CARDS

Let's face it: getting kids to do their chores can be tiresome. The constant prodding, the endless checks for progress, the stalling and bickering. It almost makes a parent want to just give up and give in.

Family chores play a significant role in building loyalty, unity, and responsibility into your child. Therefore parents must find a way to work through the agony for the future rewards. Connie Hadidian, author of *Creative Family Times* (Moody Press), offers a creative approach to accomplishing family chores for children of *Childwise* age and younger.[16]

You'll need colored 3x5 index cards, an index card box, 3x5 dividers, and a black marker.

Divide your chore card box into four sections. Pick one color to use for each child's personal tasks (Blue for Billy's personal tasks, red for Rachel's). Personal chores include making the bed, brushing teeth, picking up the child's room, etc. Choose another color to represent chores that all children are capable of doing, e.g., sweeping the kitchen floor, emptying the trash can, wiping down the sliding door, folding the laundry, and so on. Use those extra cards (the purple ones) for special "See Mom for a treat" cards.

Here is how it works for one child. Each morning, Matthew's chore cards are placed out for him on the kitchen table or the counter. This will consist of his blue cards (personal tasks) and some green cards (anybody tasks). Mom sets the timer on the microwave for an appropriate amount of time. Matthew works through his cards, flipping each face down when the task is completed until all chores are done. They must all be done before the timer goes off.

Some cards are for chores that must be done daily. Others are for weekly or monthly chores, such as taking sheets off the bed, cleaning out desk drawers, and sweeping the patio. Some of the weekly or monthly chores should be given after school and not during the regular chore time.

The last card in Michael's stack reads, "See Mom if you think you are done." This card is helpful for two reasons. First, it lets you know if the chores are done before the timer goes off, and second, you can check to see if the job is done to your satisfaction.

Every once in a while, mom throws in the special card: "See Mom for a treat." When the children discover this, and after their squeals of delight die down, express your appreciation for how well they are doing. The special treat might be going out for ice cream, going out to a restaurant, or receiving a dollar bill.

If you have young children who do not read yet, put a picture on the index card to represent the chore. A bed or a toy box. You might even use this as an opportunity to introduce simple words.

For example, draw a picture of a bed and above it, write, "Make bed." For the little ones, it takes about a week before they are doing their chores independently and successfully.

Here are some advantages to this method:

1. It takes only a few minutes each morning to gather the children's chore cards for the day.

2. It teaches the children responsibility and self-discipline.

3. Younger children can participate.

4. The system is flexible. You can add or delete chores as needed and as the child grows older.

Finally, regarding motivation, remember that simply getting outward performance is not the goal of your parenting, but the goal is to help create a servant's heart in your children. Chores are one way to teach the virtue of *otherness*. Your children need to feel they are important, contributing members of your family. Having them do chores is one way to accomplish this.

CHARTING POSITIVE ACTION

By using the principles in *Childwise*, we believe you will begin to see progress in the correction arena. However, sometimes we all need something a little extra. The positive action chart is a nifty tool that can move a child from the not-doing-wrong stage into the spontaneously-doing-right stage.

This calls for the creation of a colorful chart. Maybe even a special trip to the craft store with your little one to purchase the needed material. Let her help—this will further enhance the experience.

Select poster board and markers and a variety of fun-filled stickers.

Before creating the chart, consider specific traits you would like to see developing in the heart of your child. Love, joy, peace, patience, kindness, goodness, faithfulness, gentleness, and self-control are good starting points. These present a well-rounded picture of a person living out the first principle.

On the left-hand column of your chart, list these attributes. List days of the week across the top. Now post this chart in a prominent place in your home. The kitchen is perfect or even the child's bedroom, if you don't mind him dragging every visitor into his room to check out the cool poster the two of you created.

Here's how it works. Each time your child demonstrates one of the positive attributes on the chart, you point it out. You explain exactly what happened and how it relates to the desirable trait. And you go put a sticker on the chart.

You may be surprised by what happens. Surprised not by how your child desires to start aiming high (though this will, indeed, happen), but surprised at all the good things your child has already been doing, but which you hadn't noticed. When you start actively looking for, say, kindness, you may find it where you least expect it. Better still will be how your child's face lights up as you begin to notice the good, inspiring actions she does everyday, more and more frequently.

For areas of development where your little one needs extra help, offer especially fantastic stickers when that trait is demonstrated. As soon as ten stickers are accumulated on the chart, a reward is given. This may be a trip to the ice cream parlor, the zoo, or whatever else creates a wonderful memory for your child to savor.

Your child won't be doing it for the reward (well, not *only* for the reward). The encouragement he receives from seeing his own virtues mount up is worth more to him than any scoop of mint chip or visit with a chimpanzee. Being recognized for a job well done is a major shot in the arm for his journey toward the kind of character any parent could be proud of.

MARBLES FOR A CAUSE

All too easily parents can slip into the correction-only mode. It seems all kids ever hear is, "No, no, no." They will learn quickly what they *can't* get away with, but do they really understand what exactly they should be doing instead? Only if they see goodness in action. They will adopt whatever kind of model you portray. Here's another idea to help you promote the positive in your house.

Get a small wicker basket and a bag of marbles. Whenever anyone catches another family member doing something virtuous, he gets a marble for the basket. When the basket is full, the family chooses something fun to do together.

Most wonderful is that the marble alone is enough immediate recognition to inspire similar behavior in the future. Do not think of this as a type of bribe. The attitudes and behaviors are ongoing training areas. The reward here comes only after the desired behavior occurs. This is far removed from the dangling-carrot approach, where the child is enticed to give the right behavior.

In fact, to avoid dependency on the reward, some ground rules must be established. First, there is to be no asking to put a marble in the basket by the person doing something in the right way. Someone else has to notice another's goodness. Second, there may be no complaining if a reward is not forthcoming. Yes, sometimes life will be unfair and our goodness will go unnoticed. But that is when you teach your children that we do good things not for the praise of another man but simply because it is right.

Before you start, you must actually consider what the desirable traits look like, in order not to overlook too many. For example, following through on a task is faithfulness. Not crying when a treasured candy is dropped and crushed in a carnival stampede is surely self-control. Playing nicely together for a prolonged period of time is a much-treasured peace. And sharing a new birthday treasure with another anxious onlooker demonstrates love.

By the way, humming over a basket of dirty socks is clearly worth a marble for joy.

SUMMARY

Whether you are teaching self-control, revving up your child's engine, or training into the heart those positive traits you desire for the life of your child, be creative. Be loving and fun, bearing in mind the principles for training presented in this book. There is a place for correction, stern admonishment, and clearly defined boundaries. Yet in weeding out the wrongs, don't neglect to plant the beautiful, watering with encouragement and praise. Then your child's heart truly will blossom.

Implement the above nifty ideas with wisdom and patience. Adapt them to suit your situation. Start with one and add on as desired. Each is backed by validated success and proven track records by parents like you, looking for an added boost in the right direction.

QUESTIONS FOR REVIEW

1. In what way does folding hands facilitate self-control?

2. Explain why chore cards expedite the process of chore time?

3. When is a positive action chart especially helpful to a parent?

4. What two rules are necessary to avoid dependency on rewards with the marble basket?

Epilogue

Two boys, ages eight and ten, were known around town for their mischievousness. They were always getting into trouble. Their parents could be assured that if any mischief occurred in their town, their two sons were some way involved. The parents were at their wit's end over the boys' public behavior.

The mother had heard of a clergyman in town who had been successful in working with troubled youth. She asked her husband what he thought about sending the boys to meet with him. He agreed, realizing that something had to be done and that they needed a power higher than their own.

The pastor agreed to meet with the boys but asked to see them individually. The eight-year-old went first. The pastor asked the boy sternly, "Young man, where is God?" The boy made no response, so the pastor repeated the question with more fervency. "Young man, where is God?" Still no answer. So the pastor raised his voice and shook his finger at the boy. "Young man, *where is God?*"

The boy bolted from the pastor's study and ran directly home, slamming himself in the closet. His older brother followed him in and asked, "What happened? What'd he do to you?"

"We're in big trouble this time," the younger brother said. "God is missing and they think we had something to do with it."

ONE THING YOU LACK

We have traveled many pages together and talked of many things. Yet one matter still remains. It has to do with your child's sense of God. We shall address this matter frankly.

We, the authors, believe in *ethical monotheism. Mono,* meaning "one," and *theo,* meaning "God." Monotheism: one God. Ethical monotheism means first that there is one God from which all morality is derived. Second, that God's ethical demand on man, religious or otherwise, is that we act decently toward one another.

The God we speak of was first revealed in the Hebrew Bible where his character is described as supranatural (above nature), personal, good, and holy. These traits are repeated in the Christian New Testament. Christian values reflect the person of God in Jesus Christ. When taught to children, such values trigger a child's consciousness of God and eternity.

We trust you have found this book to be helpful. Yet we believe that, apart from a personal knowledge and relationship with God through Jesus Christ, the fullness and purpose of life will always be in question, and the reality and hope for a secure future will always be in doubt.

So we, like the clergyman above, ask you, "Where is God in your life?" He is not that far away, according to the prophet Jeremiah: "You will seek me and find me when you seek me with all your heart."[17]

Seek him and he will find you.

INDEX

Accountability phase 176
Activity overload 25
Age, Respect for 97
Assumptions 17
Authority 45
    coercive 51
    parental 47
    principle-centered 50
    rule-centered 50
Authoritarian parents 47
Apologize 137

Behavioral ownership 173
Bribing parent 207

Character 64
Cheating 234
Child-centered ethic 21
Child-centered parenting 23
Childhood capacities 66
Childishness 132
Choice, addicted to 162
Choices 157
Chores 244
Coaching phase 56
Community 54
Confucius 68
Consequences
    logical 209
    natural 214
Context 83
Correction, laws of 129
Couch time 38

Defiance. 132
Democratic parenting. 53
Discipline. 115
Discipline phase. 55
Dishonesty. 230
Dignity, surrendering with 228
Dreikers, Rudolf. 53

Eating 153
Encouragement 199
Ethical monotheism. 254

Fear. 21
First principle 68
Five-minute warning 121
Food 152
Friendship phase 57
Freedoms. 157
    physical. 167
    verbal 167
Folding hands 238
Forgiveness 138
Frustration tantrums 227
Funnel concept 154

Gessell, Arnold 53
Goal charts 248
Goal incentives 205
Goals of parenting 31, 50, 54, 135, 143, 211, 246
Growth and learning 150

Heart training 114
Hume, David. 21
Honor 97
Husband/wife relationship 36

Instruction, principles of 175
Interrupt courtesy 99
Isolation. 216

Judeo-Christian ethic 53

Labor. 95
Legalism 85
Logical consequences 209, 216
Lying. 230

Marbles 248
Marriage 36
Monkeys 177
Monotheism, ethical. 254
Moral courtesies. 191
Moral diversity. 63
Moral education 76
Moral reciprocity 68
Moral training 68
Mr. and Mrs. 102

Natural consequences 214

Pal versus parents 53
Peer pressure 72, 183
Permissive parenting 22
Personality types 91
Phases of parenting 55
Power struggles 228
Pre-accountabilty phase 176
Prevention 149
Property, respect for 92

Reading. 243
Reflective sit-time. 186

Reinforcement training. 201
Repentance 187
Restitution. 141
Respect for
    age 97
    peers and siblings 103
    property 92
Rewards. 207

Self-esteem. 71
Sibling conflict. 104
Sit-time, reflective 186
Shyness 101
Sleep 151
Spanking. 213
Stealing 233
Surrendering with dignity 228

Tantrums
    temper 225
    frustration. 227
Tattling 105
Temperament. 91
Temper tantrums. 225
Training
    accountability 176
    preaccountability 176
Training phase. 56
Threatening/repeating parent 120
Three candy speed. 241

Verbal affirmation. 202
Verbal admonishment 208, 219
Verbal responses. 122

Warning, five-minute 121
Whining 224
Wise in own eyes 156
Whole child parenting 65

Yes, mom/dad 122

Notes

1. From an incident reported by Frank Koch in *Proceedings,* the Naval Institute magazine, quoted by Christian Overman, *Assumptions That Affect Our Lives* (Chatsworth, Calif.: Micah 6:8 Publishing, 1996), 14.

2. David Hume (1739–40), *A Treatise of Human Nature.* E. C. Mosner, ed. (Hammondworth, England: Penguin, 1969).

3. Rudolf Dreikers, *The Courage to Be Imperfect* (New York: Hawthorn Books, 1978), 312.

4. When we ask parents to consider the context of the moment, we are not suggesting they base their ethics on the situation (situational ethics) or that there is no absolute guide for morality (moral relativism). Adherents of these systems reject the idea of fixed moral reference points. We teach *contextual ethics,* meaning that we adapt the application of fixed morality to diverse situations. Right or wrong doesn't change, but how parents apply right and wrong to life's situations ought to be flexible.

5. Genesis 4:3–4.

6. Exodus 20:15, KJV.

7. Proverbs 18:17.

8. Proverbs 29:17.

9. See Exodus 22, verses 1, 3, 5, 6, and 12.

10. See the New Testament story of the repentant Jewish tax collector Zacchaeus, Luke 19:1–8. In his repentant statement to Jesus, Zacchaeus said, "If I have cheated anybody out of anything, I will pay back four times the amount" (v. 8). This was restitution according to the law.

11. *Journal of Developmental and Behavorial Pediatrics,* 1999, 20:29–33. Cf. "Children Who Sleep Less 'Act Out' More," *Reuters Health,* Families for Early Autism Treatment, daily online newsletter, 15 June 1999. See www.feat.org.

12. Proverbs 16:24.

13. Romans 16:18.

14. For those seeking more guidance on the proper use of spanking as a tool of discipline, consider entering the course entitled *Growing Kids God's Way.* Classes are hosted by local churches and most denominations, and offered in many communities around the country.

15. Bill Bennett, *Book of Virtues* (New York: Simon & Schuster, 1993), 12.

16. Allan and Connie Hadidian, *Creative Family Times* (Chicago: Moody Press, 1989).

17. Jeremiah 29:13.